Build Your Own
ENTERTAINMENT CENTERS

Build Your Own
ENTERTAINMENT CENTERS

ANDY SCHULTZ

POPULAR WOODWORKING BOOKS

Cincinnati, Ohio

Read This Important Safety Notice

To prevent accidents, keep safety in mind while you work. Use the safety guards installed on power equipment; they are for your protection. When working on power equipment, keep fingers away from saw blades, wear safety goggles to prevent injuries from flying wood chips and sawdust, wear ear protection to protect your hearing, and consider installing a dust vacuum to reduce the amount of airborne sawdust in your woodshop. Don't wear loose clothing, such as neckties or shirts with loose sleeves, or jewelry, such as rings, necklaces or bracelets, when working on power equipment, and tie back long hair to prevent it from getting caught in your equipment. People who are sensitive to certain chemicals should check the chemical content of any product before using it. The author and editors who compiled this book have tried to make all the contents as accurate and correct as possible. Plans, illustrations, photographs and text have been carefully checked. All instructions, plans and projects should be carefully read, studied and understood before beginning construction. Due to the variability of local conditions, construction materials, skill levels, etc., neither the authors nor Popular Woodworking Books assumes any responsibility for any accidents, injuries, damages or other losses incurred resulting from the material presented in this book.

A Word About Dimensions

The author and editors who compiled the information for this book have gone over all of the dimensions, drawings, photographs, text and captions to ensure that the information here is accurate. The best woodworkers plan projects through before they cut the first piece of wood. Please take the time to go over all of the dimensions for your project whether you are designing your own or building a project straight out of the book. This practice will not only ensure that you do not waste any wood, but will give you a unique understanding and appreciation of the furniture you are about to build.

Other fine Popular Woodworking Books are available from your local bookstore or direct from the publisher.

02 01 00 99 98   6 5 4 3 2

Library of Congress Cataloging-in-Publication Data

Schultz, Andy.
Build your own entertainment centers/by Andy Schultz.
p. cm.
Includes index.
ISBN 1-55870-436-1 (alk. paper)
1. Entertainment centers (Cabinetwork)—Amateurs' manuals. 2. Recreation rooms—Equipment and supplies—Amateurs' manuals. I. Title.
TT197.5.E5S38
684.1'6—dc21   96-52651
                                                          CIP

Editor: R. Adam Blake
Content Editor: Bruce Stoker
Production Editor: Jennifer Lepore
Cover and Interior Designer: Chad Planner
Cover Photographer: Roger D. Barnes Photography

METRIC CONVERSION CHART		
TO CONVERT	**TO**	**MULTIPLY BY**
Inches	Centimeters	2.54
Centimeters	Inches	0.4
Feet	Centimeters	30.5
Centimeters	Feet	0.03
Yards	Meters	0.9
Meters	Yards	1.1
Sq. Inches	Sq. Centimeters	6.45
Sq. Centimeters	Sq. Inches	0.16
Sq. Feet	Sq. Meters	0.09
Sq. Meters	Sq. Feet	10.8
Sq. Yards	Sq. Meters	0.8
Sq. Meters	Sq. Yards	1.2
Pounds	Kilograms	0.45
Kilograms	Pounds	2.2
Ounces	Grams	28.4
Grams	Ounces	0.04

ABOUT THE AUTHOR

Andy Schultz is a master woodworker who has designed and built projects for many national woodworking magazines. Andy is a novelist, former professor at California State University at San Bernadino, former book editor for Taunton Press, and a freelance writer for *Popular Woodworking, Woodworker, Fine Homebuilding* and *Fine Woodworking* magazines. He lives, works wood and writes in Lincoln, Nebraska.

ACKNOWLEDGMENTS

To Adam Blake, Bruce Woods, Steve Shanesy and Cristine Antolik; thanks for your encouragement and faith that I could pull this off. Many thanks to my wife, Mary Sutton, and my two kids, Andrew and Nichole, for their willingness to put up with a grumpy husband and dad. I'll make it all up to you now. Many thanks to Jack and Lorraine Sutton for looking after the kids and supporting their shiftless son-in-law beyond all common sense and reason. And finally, anything good I have finally managed to do here, I owe to my dad, Lumir Schultz. He took me into the shop at four years old, and I've been welcome there ever since. Most of the other establishments I'm known at have cut me off altogether.

TABLE OF CONTENTS

Here are the designs, dimensions and construction steps for you to build the armoire-style, secretary-style or three-piece entertainment center of your choice.

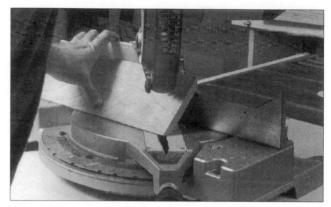

Maybe your decor requires an entertainment center that is just a bit more refined; learn how to build elegant frame-and-panel and raised panel cabinets from solid wood. Or maybe your living room cannot accommodate a center spanning an entire wall; learn how to build your cabinet to fit in a corner.

Cabinet doors provide more than mere access to the electronic treasures within. They are the focal point of your entertainment center and provide some of the most important vehicles to carry the chosen style motif to the viewer.

An entertainment center organizes your entertainment equipment, but what about all those accessories? You need a place to store your audio and video tapes, CDs and video games; learn how to build sturdy drawers to store and organize your collections.

Even though you've got a choice of four design styles, the hardware to make your entertainment center is universal. Choose from a variety of hinges, drawer and extension slides and organizers to make your center sturdy and accessible.

TABLE OF CONTENTS

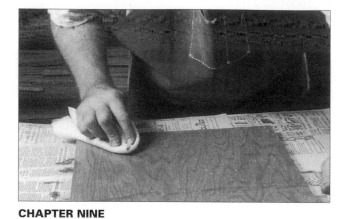

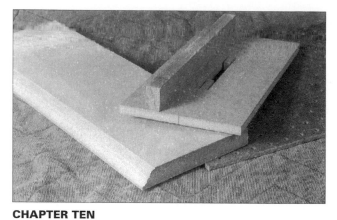

INTRODUCTION

My family loves television and we rent movies almost every weekend. My kids are budding musicians and love to tape their musical progress as well as listen to music through our sound system. We're a computer family, too, and my son's online at every opportunity, his nimble fingers dancing through websites. We do all the games as well—Nintendo, computer games, board games, word games, card games and just game games. Got the picture? We've got lots of entertainment stuff, stacks of stereo gear, boxes of tapes, cassettes, CDs, videos and other electronics stuff that need a home, a site, (dare I say it?) a shrine.

I had been drooling over entertainment centers for some time, but sticker shock and the abysmal quality of good cabinetry kept me from buying. When a customer began making inquiries about building an entertainment center for her home, I had an optimistic thought—maybe I can make one for my family at the same time. I called Steve Shanesy at *Popular Woodworking* to talk about writing an article for them to further defray building costs. Steve turned me on to Adam Blake at Betterway Books, who thought, "Maybe there's a book in it." That was just a year ago. Over a three-month period, Adam helped me hone my ideas into a proposal that featured an array of twelve different styles of furniture. We wanted a book that would enable just about anyone with a modest home shop to succeed at building an entertainment center. There was only one catch—I had to build three sets of cabinets in three different styles.

In about nine months, I built three entertainment centers and wrote this book; however, I don't believe building any of these will take you that long. It should take you between 160 and 200 hours to complete any of these projects. While the monetary costs are substantial, I believe you will be able to build an entertainment center for roughly half of what it costs to buy the best cabinetry. (Don't compare with the cut-rate places—you'll never be able to beat their prices, and if you are drawn to that sort of furniture, don't even consider building.)

One of the things Adam and I haggled over was the question of style. What kind of furniture are people drawn to? What are the features we need to incorporate into these designs? Gradually, the plans for several sorts of entertainment centers evolved. Essentially, we looked at sort of small, medium and large formats for entertainment centers in country, mission, Shaker and contemporary styles.

HOW THIS BOOK IS ORGANIZED

The central idea of this book is that you should be able to build any of the styles in any of the configurations if I show you how to build one of each configuration. Consequently, in the first section of the book, Projects, I cover how to build specific projects. In the first chapter I show you how to build the medium configuration entertainment center, the wardrobe on chest or armoire, in the country style. In the second chapter, I build a small configuration entertainment center, a secretary in the mission style. In chapter three, I build a large configuration entertainment center, a three-piece entertainment center in the Shaker style.

Because these entertainment centers are built from many identical components, the second section of the book, Techniques, reveals generic techniques that apply to all twelve entertainment centers. Thus, in chapter four, plywood carcass building is detailed; in chapter six, drawer making; in eight, hardware selection and installation, and so on. Study the table of contents to familiarize yourself with the organization of the book, and then pore over the pictures in each chapter to get a broad idea of how the book has been designed. You are not expected to use this book sequentially from page 1 through page 128. Rather, go from the plans in chapter one, two or three, to chapter four to build the carcasses, to chapter seven to build the doors, etc. Finally, when all needed components are built, return to chapter one, two or three to complete the project within that particular style and configuration.

WHAT EQUIPMENT DO I NEED?

When I said you need a modest workshop, I meant you absolutely must have a table saw and a bunch of hand tools and portable power tools. Certainly, you must have both a plunge router and a fixed-base router. I like the Porter-Cable model 690 router because you can get a plunge router base for it and thereby get two good routers for a relatively low price. You'll need a power drill, saber saw and biscuit joiner. As a minimum you'll need a high-quality jack plane, a block plane, a combination square and a router table setup for your router. You'll also need a high-quality straightedge.

Although they are not absolutely needed, I made extensive use of my lightweight portable planer, my 8" jointer, my drill press and bandsaw. My radial arm saw was extremely handy for breaking down big lumber into smaller pieces. My 14.4 volt cordless drill is without a doubt one of my most used tools. Can you get by without each of these tools? Of course, but time is usually the victim in these compromises between pocketbook and time clock.

Undoubtedly, and in addition to those you will build or borrow, you will need to buy several jigs, bits, guides and other accessories for your tools and machines. In everything but underwear and umbrellas, buy the best you can afford. My logic: You're gonna lose the umbrella anyway, and with the underwear, who's gonna know? Good luck with your project.

MAKING ARMOIRE-STYLE ENTERTAINMENT CENTERS

The drawings and building sequence at the end of the chapter detail how to build four different styles of this wardrobe on chest or armoire. If you've decided an armoire is the right size for your room, determine which style will look best in your house. Study the drawings and materials list. After reading chapter ten, figure out how much of what you'll need to complete this project, and order the materials from local suppliers, or order them from some of the suppliers listed in the back of the book. Similarly, study the hardware needed to complete the project, browse through chapter eight and order the hardware from some of the suppliers listed in the back of the book or buy it locally.

After your materials and hardware arrive, begin building. Go first to chapters four and five and plot how you're going to build the needed carcasses for this project. After the plywood carcasses are built, study the steps in face-frame construction detailed in chapter two on page 49 and attach the face frames to your cabinets. (Face frames are not needed for contemporary-style entertainment centers.)

Now build the drawers and doors, chapters six and seven, and then install the hardware, chapter eight. Finish the components as per chapter nine, and now read the remainder of this chapter to complete your project.

Country-Style Armoire

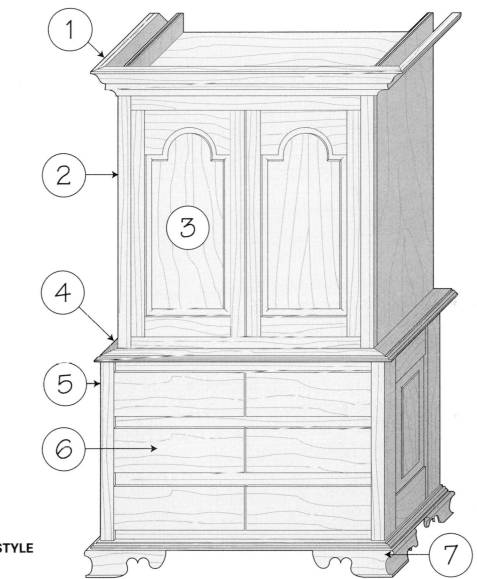

**FIGURE 1-1:
COUNTRY-STYLE
ARMOIRE**

SUBASSEMBLY LIST—COUNTRY-STYLE ARMOIRE		
No.	**Subassembly**	**Refer to**
1	Pediment	Building sequence on page 51, exploded drawings on page 14.
2	Upper Carcass and Face Frame	Building sequence on pages 49 & 74, exploded drawings on page 14.
3	Country-Style Doors	Building sequence in chapter 6, exploded drawings on page 15.
4	Counter and Base	Building sequence on page 30, exploded drawings on page 16.
5	Lower Carcass	Building sequence on page 26, exploded drawings on page 18.
6	Drawer	Building sequence in chapter 7, exploded drawings on page 19.
7	Country-Style Foot	Building sequence on page 28, exploded drawings on page 17.

Pediment
DIMENSIONS

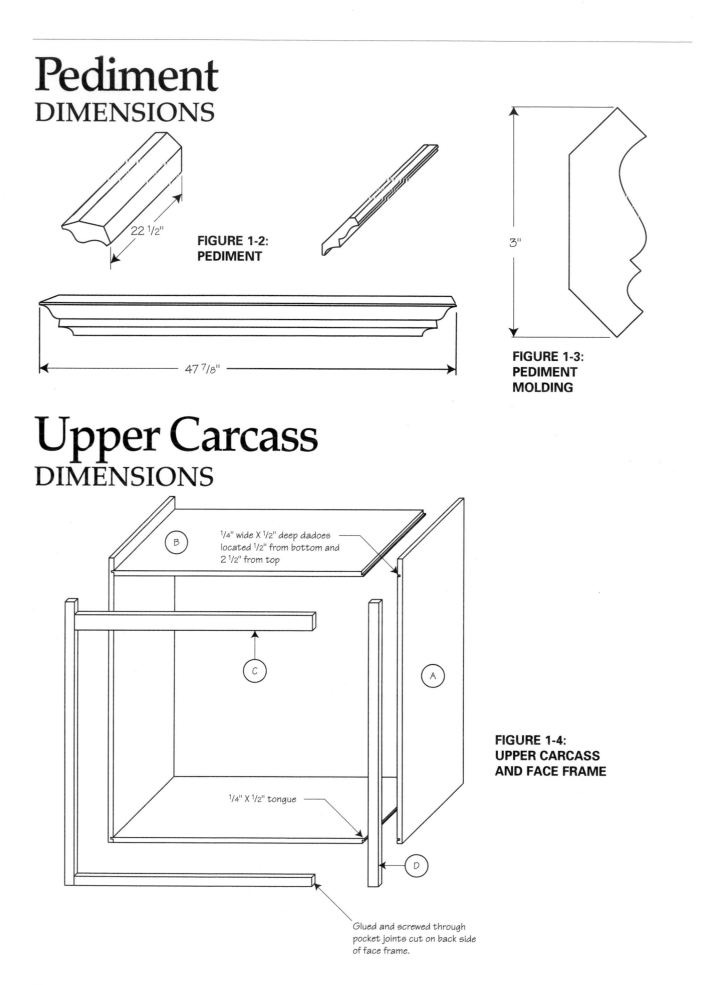

22 1/2"

**FIGURE 1-2:
PEDIMENT**

3"

**FIGURE 1-3:
PEDIMENT
MOLDING**

47 7/8"

Upper Carcass
DIMENSIONS

B

1/4" wide X 1/2" deep dadoes
located 1/2" from bottom and
2 1/2" from top

C

A

**FIGURE 1-4:
UPPER CARCASS
AND FACE FRAME**

1/4" X 1/2" tongue

D

Glued and screwed through
pocket joints cut on back side
of face frame.

Door
DIMENSIONS

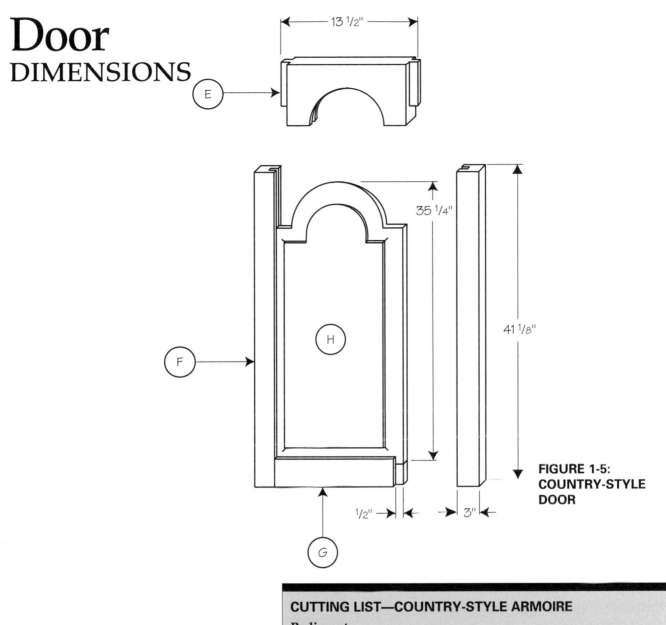

13 ½"

E

35 ¼"

F

H

41 ⅛"

G

½"

3"

**FIGURE 1-5:
COUNTRY-STYLE
DOOR**

CUTTING LIST—COUNTRY-STYLE ARMOIRE

Pediment

Pediment Molding		¾" x 3" x 96"	Maple
Upper Carcass			
(A) Carcass Side	(2)	¾" x 22¼" x 43½"	Birch Plywood
(B) Top & Bottom	(2)	¾" x 22¼" x 42¼"	Birch Plywood
(C) Face-Frame Sides	(2)	¾" x 2" x 43½"	Maple
(D) Face-Frame Crosspieces	(2)	¾" x 2" x 38¾"	Maple
Country-Style Door			
(E) Upper Rail	(2)	¾" x 6" x 13½"	Maple
(F) Stile	(4)	¾" x 3" x 41⅛"	Maple
(G) Lower Rail	(2)	¾" x 3½" x 13½"	Maple
(H) Panel	(2)	¾" x 13½" x 35¼"	Maple

Counter and Base
DIMENSIONS

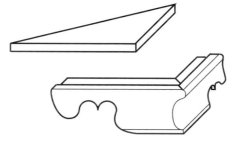

FIGURE 1-6:
COUNTER, BASE
AND FOOT
ASSEMBLY

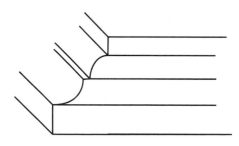

Molding profile, full size

FIGURE 1-7:
COUNTER AND
BASE MOLDING
PROFILE

CUTTING LIST—COUNTRY-STYLE ARMOIRE			
Counter and Base			
(I) Side	(4)	¼" x 5" x 26"	Maple
(J) Front	(2)	¼" x 5" x 47"	Maple
(K) Center Panel	(2)	¼" x 22" x 37"	Medium-Density Fiberboard (MDF)
Foot			
Foot	(6)	⅜" x 5" x 10½"	Maple

Foot
DIMENSIONS

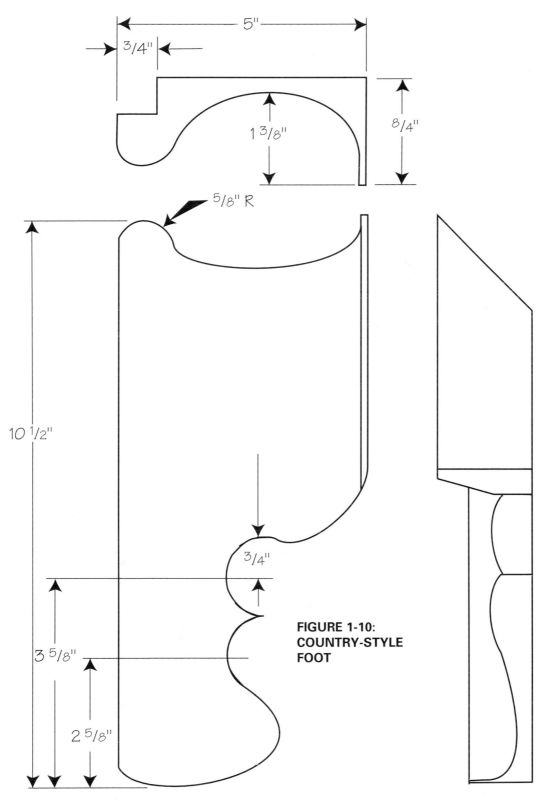

5"

3/4"

8/4"

1 3/8"

5/8" R

10 1/2"

3/4"

**FIGURE 1-10:
COUNTRY-STYLE
FOOT**

3 5/8"

2 5/8"

Lower Carcass
DIMENSIONS

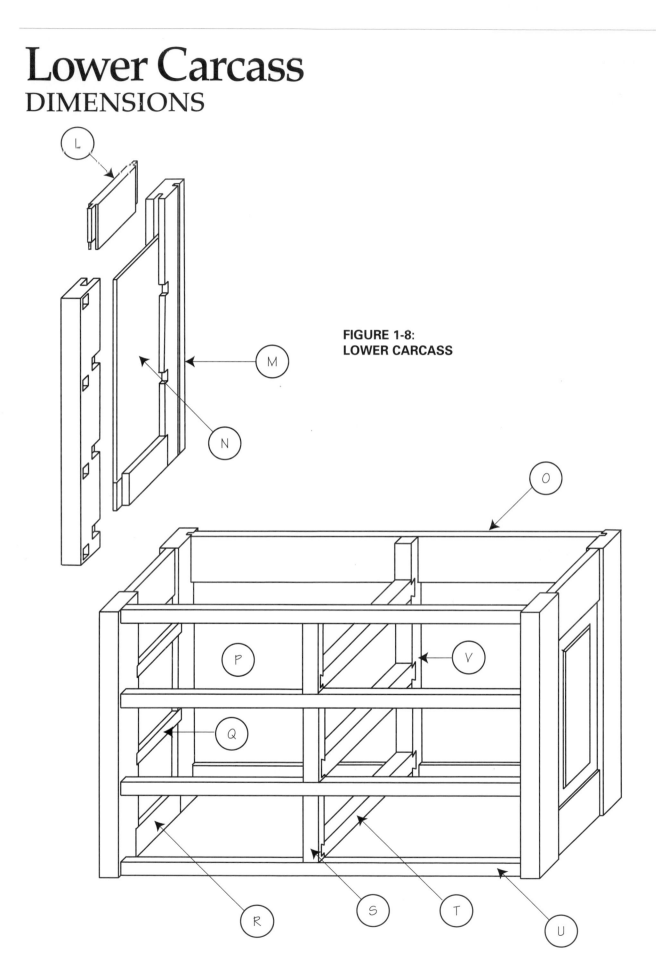

FIGURE 1-8:
LOWER CARCASS

Drawer
DIMENSIONS

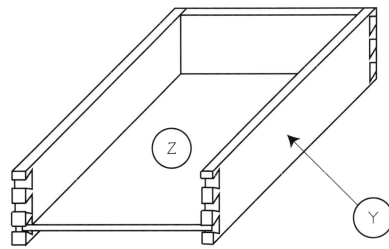

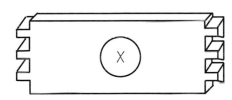

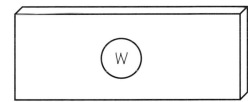

FIGURE 1-9:
DRAWER

CUTTING LIST—COUNTRY-STYLE ARMOIRE

Lower Carcass

(L) Side Rail	(4)	¾" x 3 ½" x 18"	Maple
(M) Carcass Stile	(4)	⅝" x 4" x 30"	Maple
(N) Side Panel	(2)	¾" x 18" x 24"	Maple
(O) Rear Stile	(2)	¾" x 3½" x 41¾"	Maple
(P) Rear Panel		¼" x 24" x 41¾"	Birch Plywood
(Q) Side Slide Support	(4)	⅝" x 2" x 22"	Maple
(R) Lower Side			
Slide Support	(2)	⅝" x 3½" x 17"	Maple
(S) Front Center Stiles	(3)	1⅛" x 1⅛" x 9¼"	Maple
(T) Center Slide Support	(3)	1⅛" x 1⅛" x 22"	Maple
(U) Front Rail	(4)	⅛" x 1⅛" x 41¾"	Maple
(V) Rear Center Stile		1⅛" x 1⅛" x 30"	Maple

Drawer

(W) Drawer Front	(6)	¾" x 7⅞" x 21"	Maple
(X) Drawer Front			
& Back	(12)	½" x 7⅞" x 19½"	Maple
(Y) Drawer Side	(12)	½" x 7⅞" x 19⅜"	Maple
(Z) Drawer Bottom	(6)	¼" x 19⅛" x 19¼"	Maple

Mission-Style Armoire

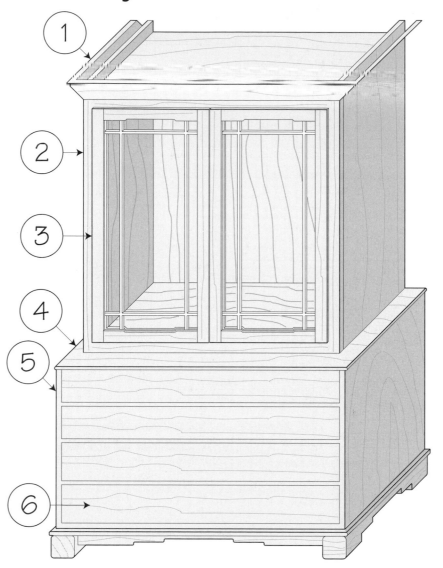

FIGURE 1-11:
MISSION-STYLE
ARMOIRE

SUBASSEMBLY LIST—MISSION-STYLE ARMOIRE

No.	Subassembly	Refer to
1	Pediment	Building sequence on page 51.
2	Upper Carcass and Face Frame	Building sequence on pages 49 & 74.
3	Mission-Style Doors	Building sequence in chapter 6.
4	Counter, Base & Feet	Building sequence on pages 28 & 30, exploded drawings on page 21.
5	Lower Carcass	Building sequence on page 26.
6	Drawer	Building sequence in chapter 7.

Counter, Base and Foot
DIMENSIONS

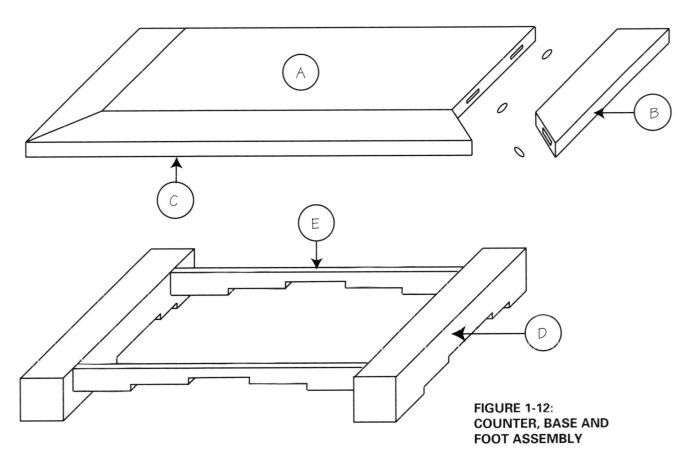

FIGURE 1-12:
COUNTER, BASE AND
FOOT ASSEMBLY

CUTTING LIST—MISSION-STYLE ARMOIRE

Counter, Base & Feet

(A) Center Panel	(2)	¾" x 22" x 37"	Medium-Density Fiberboard (MDF)
(B) Side	(4)	¾" x 5" x 26"	Oak
(C) Front	(2)	¾" x 5" x 47"	Oak
(D) Feet	(2)	1²⁄₁₂" x 1²⁄₁₂" x 24"	Oak
(E) Crosspiece	(2)	¾" x 2" x 39"	Oak

Shaker-Style Armoire

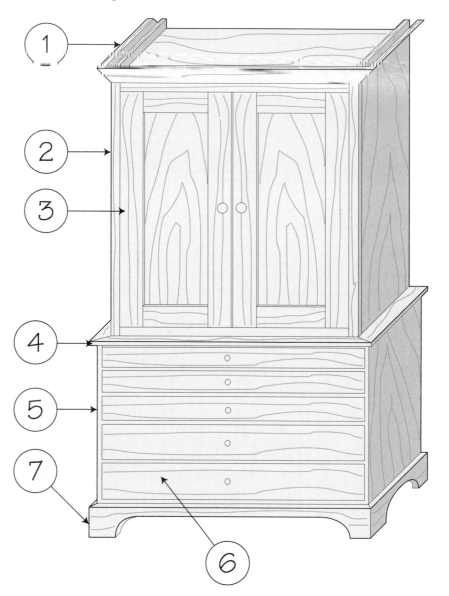

**FIGURE 1-13:
SHAKER-STYLE
ARMOIRE**

SUBASSEMBLY LIST—SHAKER-STYLE ARMOIRE

No.	Subassembly	Refer to
1	Pediment	Building sequence on page 51.
2	Upper Carcass and Face Frame	Building sequence on pages 49 & 74.
3	Shaker-Style Doors	Building sequence in chapter 6.
4	Counter	Building sequence on page 30.
5	Lower Carcass	Building sequence on page 26.
6	Drawer	Building sequence in chapter 7.
7	Foot	Building sequence on page 28, exploded drawings on page 23.

Base and Foot
DIMENSIONS

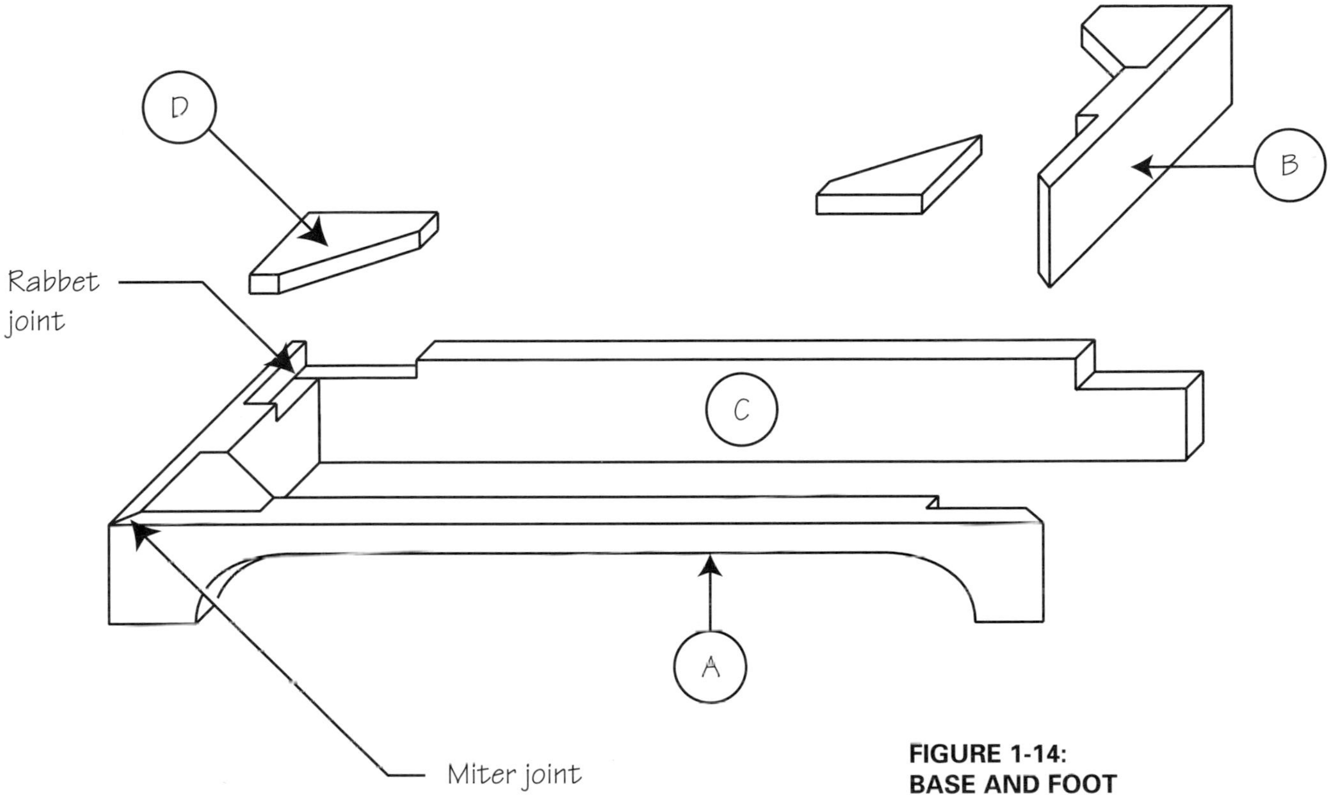

D
B
Rabbet joint
C
A
Miter joint

**FIGURE 1-14:
BASE AND FOOT**

CUTTING LIST—SHAKER-STYLE ARMOIRE

Base and Feet

(A) Front		8/4" x 5" x 46¾"	Cherry
(B) Sides	(2)	8/4" x 5" x 23"	Cherry
(C) Back		¾" x 5" x 45¼"	Cherry
(D) Gusset	(4)	¾" x 10" x 10"	Cherry Plywood

Contemporary-Style Armoire

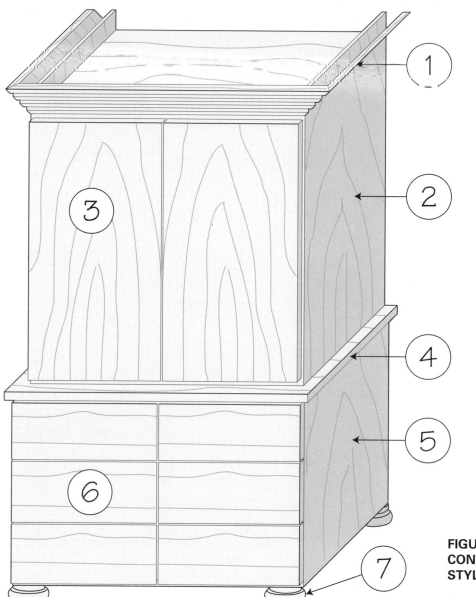

FIGURE 1-15: CONTEMPORARY-STYLE ARMOIRE

SUBASSEMBLY LIST—CONTEMPORARY-STYLE ARMOIRE

No.	Subassembly	Refer to
1	Pediment	Building sequence on page 51.
2	Upper Carcass	Building sequence on page 74.
3	Doors	Edge plywood doors with hardwood strips as shown in chapter 4.
4	Counter	Building sequence on page 30.
5	Lower Carcass	Building sequence on page 26, exploded drawings on page 25.
6	Drawer	Building sequence in chapter 7.
7	Foot	Drawing on page 25.

Lower Carcass and Foot
DIMENSIONS

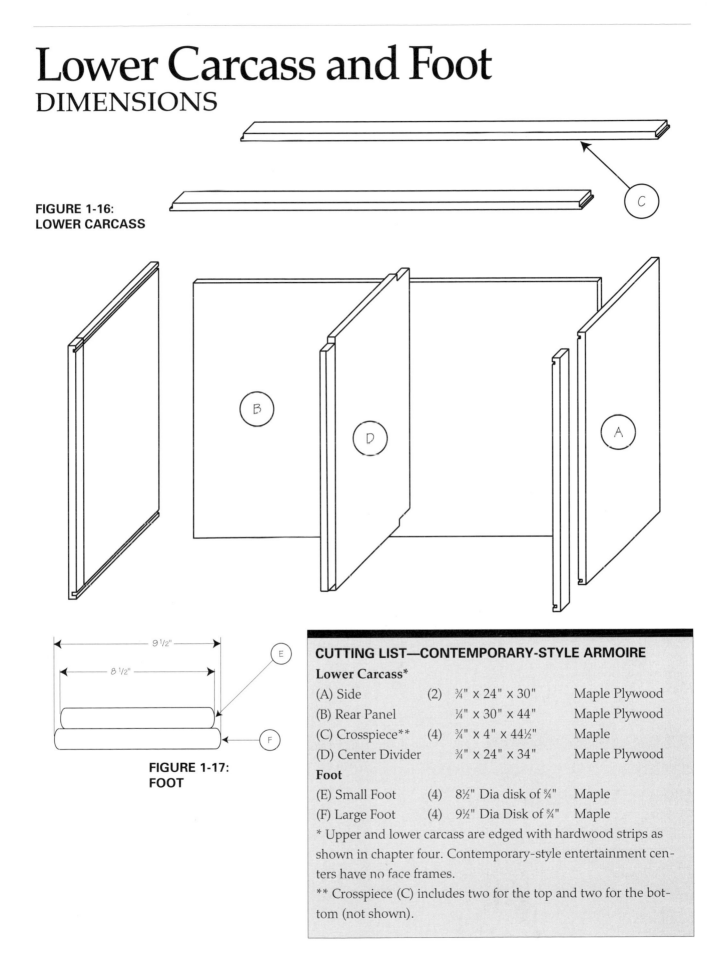

**FIGURE 1-16:
LOWER CARCASS**

**FIGURE 1-17:
FOOT**

CUTTING LIST—CONTEMPORARY-STYLE ARMOIRE

Lower Carcass*

(A) Side	(2)	¾" x 24" x 30"	Maple Plywood
(B) Rear Panel		¼" x 30" x 44"	Maple Plywood
(C) Crosspiece**	(4)	¾" x 4" x 44½"	Maple
(D) Center Divider		¾" x 24" x 34"	Maple Plywood

Foot

(E) Small Foot	(4)	8½" Dia disk of ¾"	Maple
(F) Large Foot	(4)	9½" Dia Disk of ¾"	Maple

* Upper and lower carcass are edged with hardwood strips as shown in chapter four. Contemporary-style entertainment centers have no face frames.

** Crosspiece (C) includes two for the top and two for the bottom (not shown).

BUILDING THE LOWER CARCASS

STEP 1

Mill the Wood

Like all machine woodworking, good cabinetmaking relies on good millwork. Here, the pile of carcass members for the country-style carcass await joinery operations.

STEP 2

Plough the Groove

Plough the groove for the panels on the table saw.

STEP 3

Cut Mortises and Tenons

As with the mortise-and-tenon joinery practices revealed in chapter five (building the mission-style frame and rail bottom carcass), use a plunge router and a medium-density fiberboard (MDF) jig to cut the mortises.

STEP 4

Cut Dovetail Tenons

Cut dovetail tenons for the inner support rails with a horizontally mounted router on the router table. Use the same router bit you used to cut the dovetail ways in the frame members.

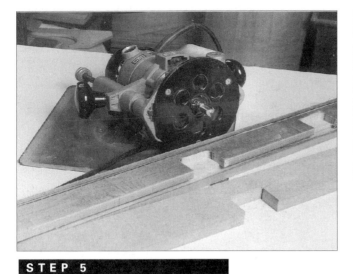

STEP 5

Make Pattern to Rout Recesses

To rout the recesses needed for the inner carcass rails, first make a pattern by cutting a square notch in a piece of ½" MDF the same width as the rail and about 1" forward.

STEP 6

Cut Recesses

Next, use a plunge router and a straight pattern bit to cut the recess. Cut it deep enough so the rail fits flush with the inner carcass rail surface.

STEP 7

Glue Up the Carcass

After the end assemblies are glued and the inner rails are glued and screwed in place, glue up the frame members and clamp the carcass with bar clamps.

STEP 8

Glue Up Inner Carcass Rails

Glue the inner carcass rails in place.

MAKING THE FEET

Cut the Cove

Cutting the feet for the country-style entertainment center requires considerable shaping. Here I'm cutting a cove by passing the workpiece over the table saw with a temporary fence clamped at an angle across the table. I initially removed much of the waste by ripping it away with a dado head. I've clamped finger boards in place to prevent kickback and to ensure the workpiece is kept in correct position. Take small cuts.

STEP 2

Cut the Miters

Once the cove is fully cut, cut the miters for the feet. If you have a sled dedicated to tilted-blade crosscuts, use it rather than the miter gauge. Use a plastic 45° right triangle to check the blade tilt prior to cutting.

STEP 3

Reverse the Miter Gauge

Reverse the miter gauge in the slot to cut a miter going the opposite direction rather than turning the workpiece over. This way, the same referent surface slides across the tabletop and the identical angle is cut.

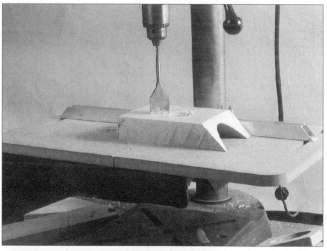

STEP 4

Trace the Pattern

After the miters are cut, trace the pattern for the foot (see drawing on page 17) on the back of each foot and draw center lines for the two holes as indicated. Now begin the inside curves of the feet by boring two tangent holes halfway through the foot with the coved surface facing down. I used a 1½" diameter spade bit.

Bore the Holes

Now reverse the foot so the coved surface is up, and use the hole where the brad point of the spade bit emerged through the foot as a guide to bore the remainder of each hole. By boring halfway through in this fashion, tear-out is minimized.

Band Saw the Pattern

Band saw out the remainder of each foot with the cove facing down to the band saw's table. Trim off excess material by ripping on the table saw, and round outside curves with a rasp.

Smooth and Shape

Sand the inner curves of the foot with sanding drums mounted in portable hand drills.

Sand the Shape

Outside curves can be sanded by hand using a flat sanding block, or mechanically as here where I've got my belt sander mounted vertically and outfitted with a homemade table.

MAKING THE BASE AND COUNTER

Cut the Miter Joints

Build the base and counter by edging a piece of MDF or plywood with hardwood. First, cut the miters for the corners. It's easy to adjust the two fences on the mitering sled to 90°—you just use a square and adjust both fences until they form a right angle. The hard part is splitting that 90° angle into two exact 45° angles. The trick to cutting perfect miters on the mitering sled is to cut one side of the miter on the left-hand fence and the right-hand side of the miter on the right-hand side of the fence. In this fashion, if one miter is 44.9° and the other is 45.1°, the miter still forms a perfect 90° angle.

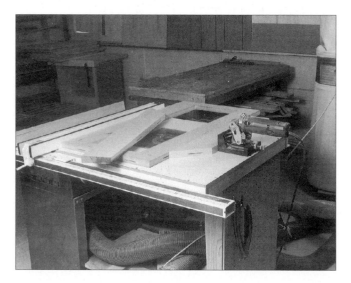

STEP 2

Biscuit Join Hardwood to Plywood Core

Once the miters are cut and the core of the base is trimmed to size, cut biscuit slots for the hardwood edging and glue up the base. Clamp with bar clamps until the glue has dried, and then surface to size if you have a planer that will accommodate these large glued up panels, or belt sand them flat.

STEP 3

Remove Excess Weight

I used ¾" plywood for the core of this cabinet base and counter for the three-piece Shaker-style entertainment center and then edged each with hardwood. (MDF would have been a cheaper alternative to the plywood.) Here I reduce the weight of the counter by raising the table saw blade up through the material and then advancing the workpiece until the endpoint of the cut has been reached. Then I lower the blade and use a saber saw to complete the cut.

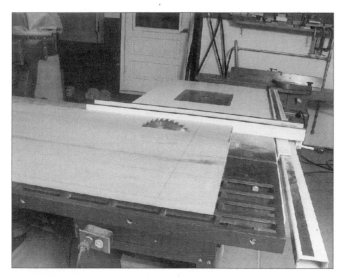

Make Pierced Cuts

To make these pierced saw cuts, first raise the table saw blade as high as possible and then move the fence right next to it. Pencil a mark on the fence at both ends of the saw blade where it emerges from the throat plate. Draw a square line across the fence from both points that you've marked. Next, extend the line from where you want to begin or stop the cut all the way across the face of the workpiece to the edge that will ride against the fence. Move the fence to the correct distance from the saw blade and position the workpiece so the back line on the workpiece is aligned with the one on the fence that marks the rear location of the saw blade when it's fully elevated. Hold the workpiece with your right hand, turn on the table saw and raise the saw blade until it is fully elevated.

Complete the Pierced Cut

Advance the saw blade into the work until the forward line aligns with the mark on the fence that shows where the front of the saw blade begins. Finally, lower the blade and turn off the machine.

INSTALLING THE ENTERTAINMENT CENTER

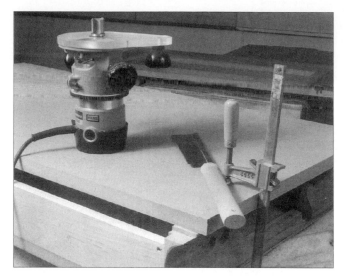

STEP 1

Notch the Feet

Notch the rear feet of the base to clear the tack strip that holds your carpet in place along the wall. I use a pattern bit in my router to follow the straightedge to rout the 5⁄16"-deep notch 1¼" wide. To eliminate the possibility of tear-out, I saw a kerf where the notch ends before routing.

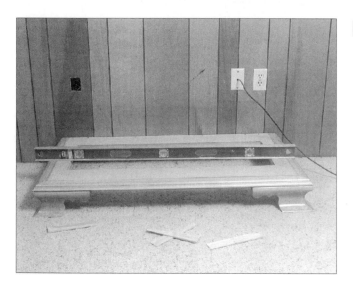

STEP 2

Level the Base

Once all wiring (video, electrical, stereo, etc.) has been routed to the area, install the base unit by checking for level, using wedges if needed, locating studs and then screwing 2½" drywall screws through the rear brace into the studs. Once level, mount the base cabinet and counter, screwing drywall screws into the foot unit and into the wall studs.

STEP 3

Install the VCR Box

Before installing the upper carcass, install the VCR box in the center cabinet with four connector screws.

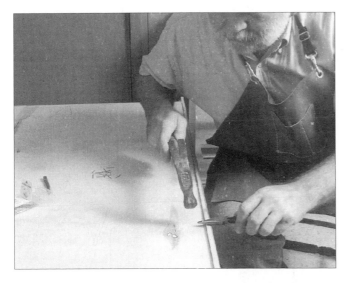

Install Plywood Back

Install the ¼" plywood back into the carcass, and nail it in place using ⅞" brads. If you have pudgy fingers, use needle-nose pliers to hold the brad before driving. Set the nailheads with a nail set. Cut venting holes and cable routing holes, as shown in chapter three on page 73, and then lift unit on top of counter and slide it into position.

Secure to Wall

Lag screw the crosspiece at the top of the cabinet carcass into wall studs with ¼" x 3½" lag screws to counter the weight of the television when it's pulled out on its swivel.

CHAPTER TWO

MAKING SECRETARY-STYLE ENTERTAINMENT CENTERS

The drawings and building sequence at the end of this chapter detail how to build four different styles of this secretary. If you've decided a secretary is the right size for your room, determine which style will look best in your house. Study the drawings and materials list. After reading chapter ten, figure out how much of what you'll need to complete this project, and order the materials from local suppliers, or order them from some of the suppliers listed in the back of the book. Similarly, study the hardware needed to complete the project, browse through chapter eight and order the hardware from some of the suppliers listed in the back of the book or buy it locally.

After your materials and hardware arrive, begin building. Go first to chapters four and five and plot how you're going to build the needed carcasses for this project. After the plywood carcasses are built, study the steps in face-frame construction detailed in this chapter on page 49, and attach the face frames to your cabinets. (Face frames are not needed for contemporary-style entertainment centers.)

Now build the drawers and doors, chapters six and seven, and then install the hardware, chapter eight. Finish the components as per chapter nine, and now read the remainder of this chapter to complete your project.

Country-Style Secretary

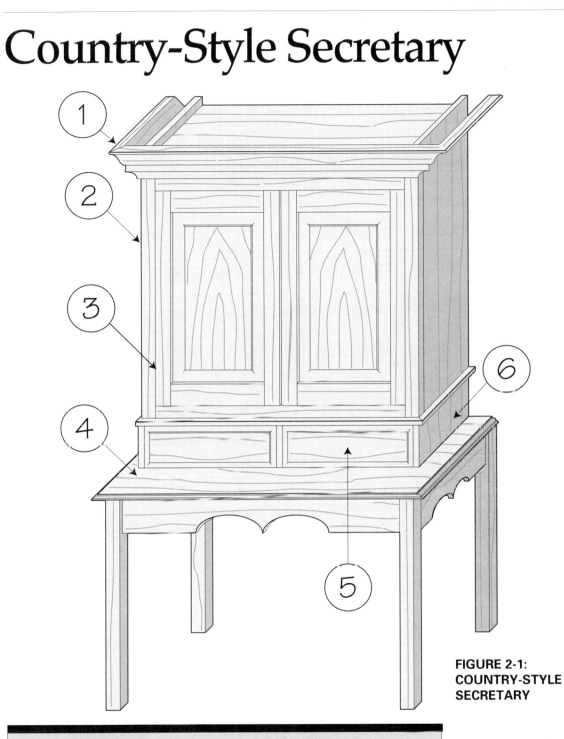

**FIGURE 2-1:
COUNTRY-STYLE
SECRETARY**

SUBASSEMBLY LIST—COUNTRY-STYLE SECRETARY

No.	Subassembly	Refer to
1	Pediment	Building sequence on page 51.
2	Upper Carcass and Face Frame	Building sequence on pages 49 & 74.
3	Country-Style Doors	Building sequence in chapter 6.
4	Table Assembly	Building sequence in chapter 5, exploded drawings on page 36.
5	Drawer	Building sequence in chapter 7.
6	Drawer Assembly	Building sequence on page 71.

Table Assembly
DIMENSIONS

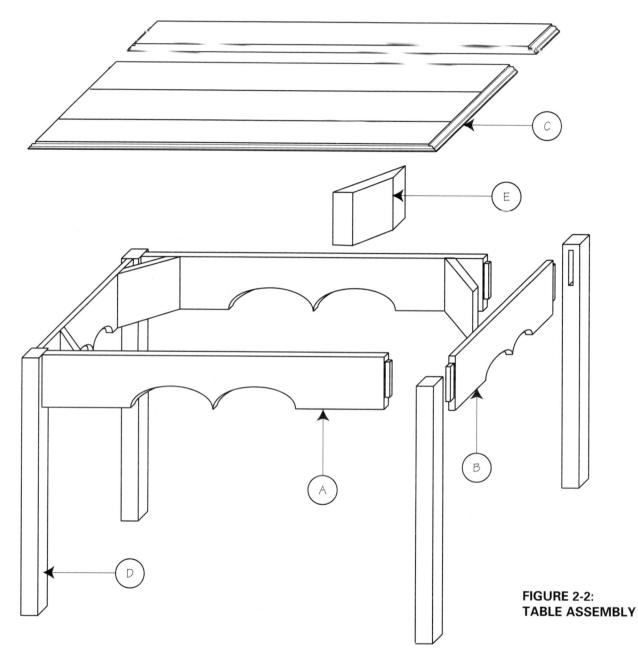

**FIGURE 2-2:
TABLE ASSEMBLY**

Mission-Style Secretary

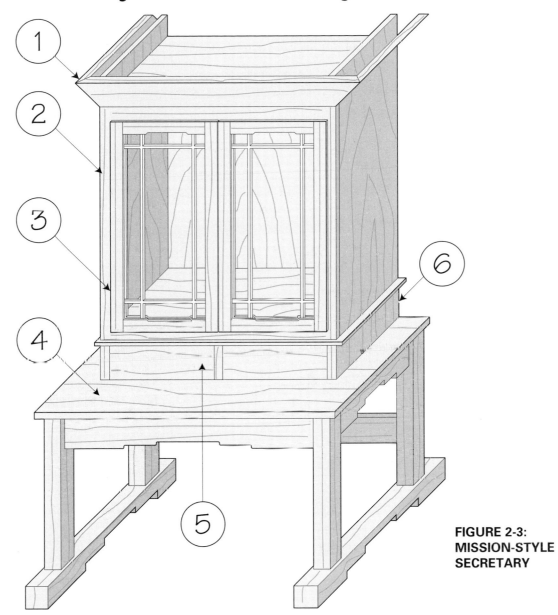

FIGURE 2-3:
MISSION-STYLE
SECRETARY

SUBASSEMBLY LIST—MISSION-STYLE SECRETARY

No.	Subassembly	Refer to
1	Pediment	Building sequence on page 51, exploded drawings on page 38.
2	Upper Carcass and Face Frame	Building sequence on pages 49 & 74, exploded drawings on page 38.
3	Mission-Style Doors	Building sequence in chapter 6, exploded drawings on page 39.
4	Table Assembly	Building sequence in chapter 5, exploded drawings on page 40.
5	Drawer	Building sequence in chapter 7, exploded drawings on page 41.
6	Drawer Assembly	Building sequence on page 71, exploded drawings on page 41.

Pediment and Upper Carcass
DIMENSIONS

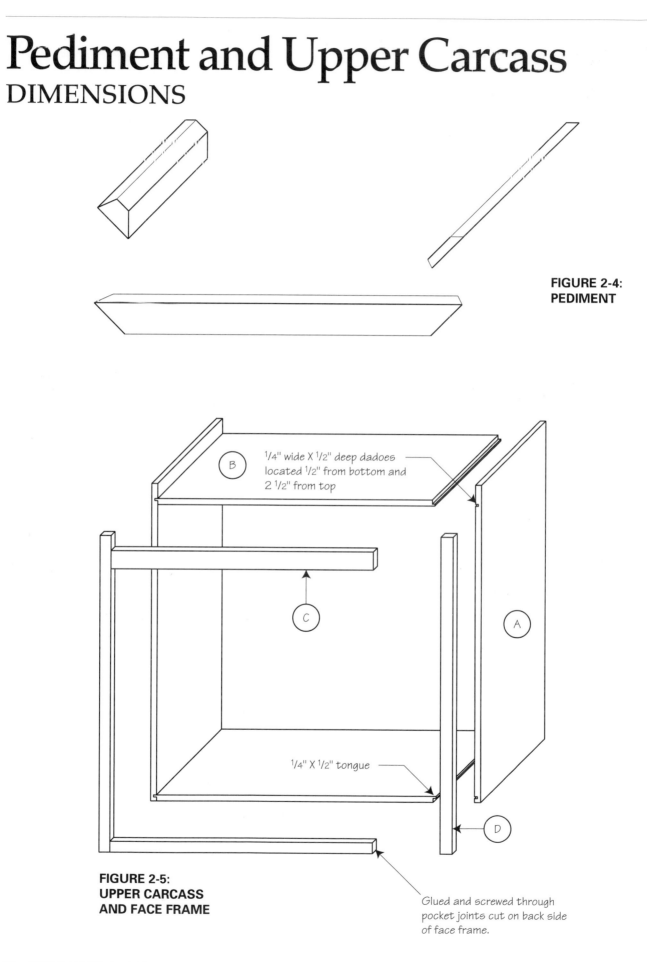

**FIGURE 2-4:
PEDIMENT**

¹/4" wide X ¹/2" deep dadoes located ¹/2" from bottom and 2 ¹/2" from top

B

C

A

¹/4" X ¹/2" tongue

D

**FIGURE 2-5:
UPPER CARCASS
AND FACE FRAME**

Glued and screwed through pocket joints cut on back side of face frame.

Door
DIMENSIONS

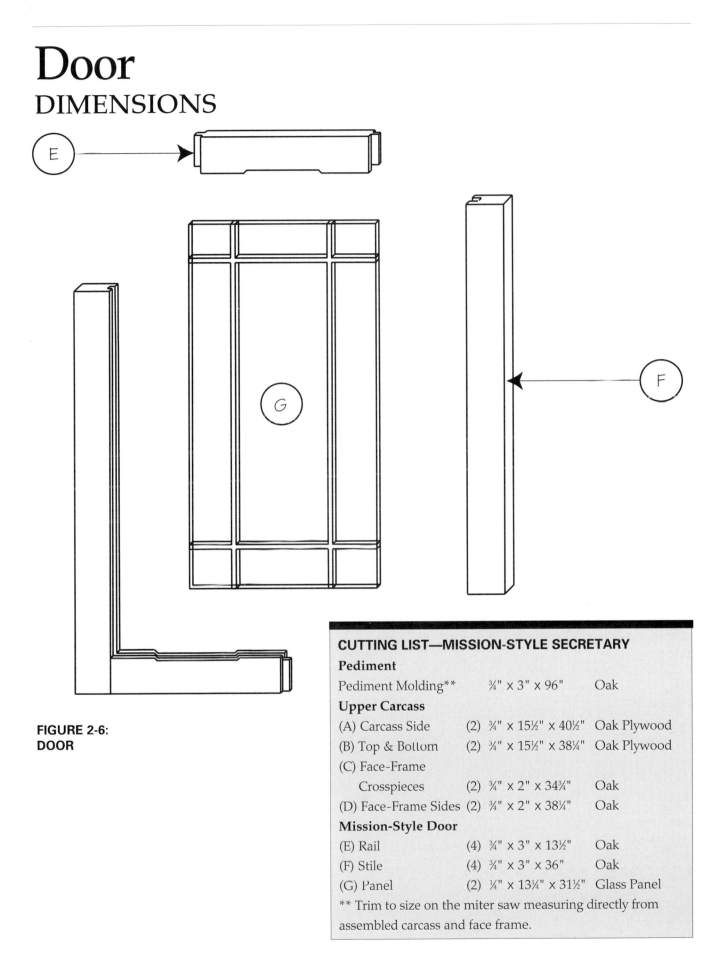

FIGURE 2-6:
DOOR

CUTTING LIST—MISSION-STYLE SECRETARY

Part		Dimensions	Material
Pediment			
Pediment Molding**		¾" x 3" x 96"	Oak
Upper Carcass			
(A) Carcass Side	(2)	¾" x 15½" x 40½"	Oak Plywood
(B) Top & Bottom	(2)	¾" x 15½" x 38¼"	Oak Plywood
(C) Face-Frame Crosspieces	(2)	¾" x 2" x 34¾"	Oak
(D) Face-Frame Sides	(2)	¾" x 2" x 38¼"	Oak
Mission-Style Door			
(E) Rail	(4)	¾" x 3" x 13½"	Oak
(F) Stile	(4)	¾" x 3" x 36"	Oak
(G) Panel	(2)	¼" x 13¼" x 31½"	Glass Panel

** Trim to size on the miter saw measuring directly from assembled carcass and face frame.

Table Assembly
DIMENSIONS

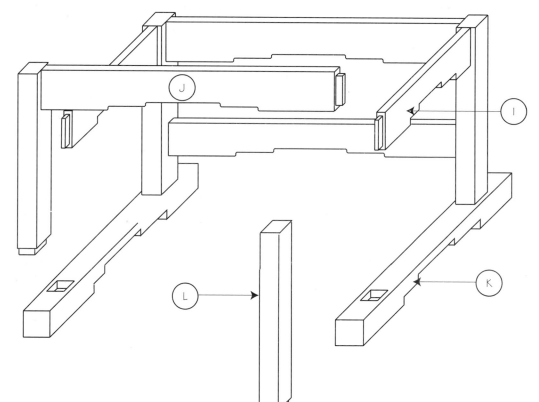

FIGURE 2-7:
TABLE ASSEMBLY

Drawer Assembly
DIMENSIONS

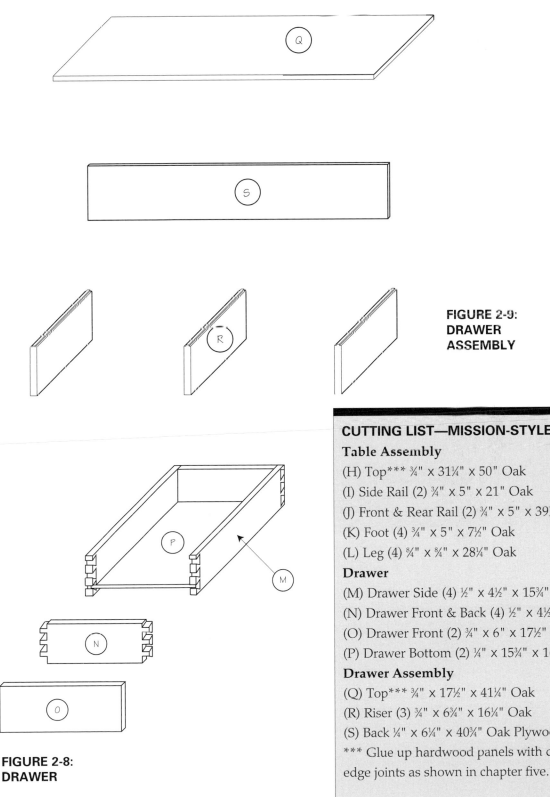

**FIGURE 2-9:
DRAWER
ASSEMBLY**

**FIGURE 2-8:
DRAWER**

CUTTING LIST—MISSION-STYLE SECRETARY

Table Assembly

(H) Top*** ¾" x 31¼" x 50" Oak

(I) Side Rail (2) ¾" x 5" x 21" Oak

(J) Front & Rear Rail (2) ¾" x 5" x 39½" Oak

(K) Foot (4) ¾" x 5" x 7½" Oak

(L) Leg (4) ⅞" x ⅞" x 28¼" Oak

Drawer

(M) Drawer Side (4) ½" x 4½" x 15¾" Oak

(N) Drawer Front & Back (4) ½" x 4½" x 16½" Oak

(O) Drawer Front (2) ¾" x 6" x 17½" Oak

(P) Drawer Bottom (2) ¼" x 15¾" x 16½" Oak

Drawer Assembly

(Q) Top*** ¾" x 17½" x 41¼" Oak

(R) Riser (3) ¾" x 6¾" x 16¼" Oak

(S) Back ¼" x 6¼" x 40¾" Oak Plywood

*** Glue up hardwood panels with dowel, biscuit or edge joints as shown in chapter five.

Shaker-Style Secretary

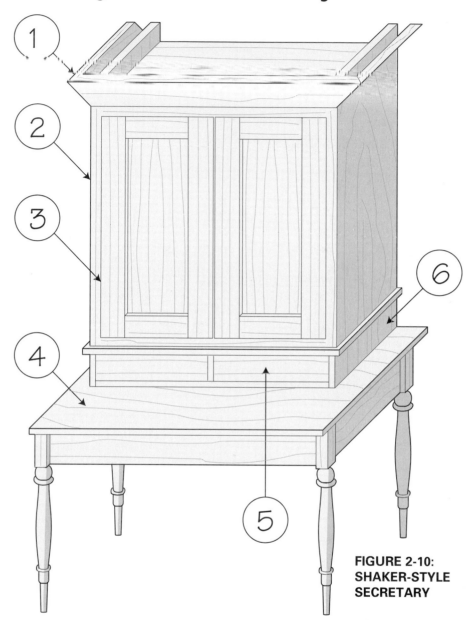

**FIGURE 2-10:
SHAKER-STYLE
SECRETARY**

SUBASSEMBLY LIST—SHAKER-STYLE SECRETARY

No.	Subassembly	Refer to
1	Pediment	Building sequence on page 51.
2	Plywood Carcass and Face Frame	Building sequence on pages 49 & 74.
3	Shaker-Style Doors	Building sequence in chapter 6.
4	Table Assembly	Building sequence in chapter 5, exploded drawings on page 43.
5	Drawer	Building sequence in chapter 7.
6	Drawer Assembly	Building sequence on page 71, exploded drawings on page 44.

Table Assembly Dimensions

DIMENSIONS

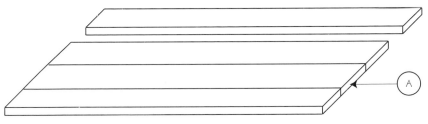

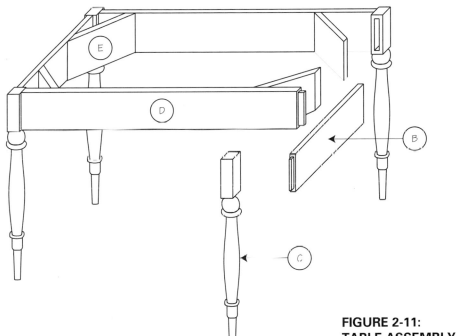

FIGURE 2-11: TABLE ASSEMBLY

CUTTING LIST—SHAKER-STYLE SECRETARY

Pediment			
Pediment Molding*		¾" x 3" x 96"	Cherry
Upper Carcass			
Carcass Side	(2)	¾" x 15½" x 40½"	Cherry Plywood
Top & Bottom	(2)	¾" x 15½" x 38¼"	Cherry Plywood
Face-Frame			
Crosspieces	(2)	¾" x 2" x 34¾"	Cherry
Face-Frame Sides	(2)	¾" x 2" x 38¼"	Cherry
Shaker-Style Door			
Rail	(4)	¾" x 3" x 13½"	Cherry
Stile	(4)	¾" x 3" x 36"	Cherry
Panel	(2)	¼" x 13¼" x 31½"	Glass

Table Assembly			
(A) Top**		¾" x 31¼" x 50"	Cherry
(B) Side Rail	(2)	¾" x 5" x 21"	Cherry
(C) Leg	(4)	8⁄4" x 8⁄4" x 28¼"	Cherry
(D) Front & Rear Rail	(2)	¾" x 5" x 39½"	Cherry
(E) Gusset	(4)	10⁄4" x 10⁄4" x 39½"	Cherry

* Trim to size on the miter saw measuring directly from assembled carcass and face frame.

** Glue up hardwood panels with dowel, biscuit or edgejoints as shown in chapter five.

Drawer Assembly
DIMENSIONS

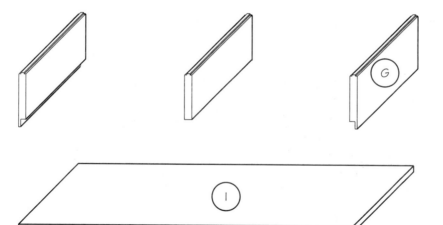

**FIGURE 2-12:
DRAWER
ASSEMBLY**

CUTTING LIST—SHAKER-STYLE SECRETARY			
Drawer			
Drawer Side	(4)	½" x 4½" x 15¾"	Cherry
Drawer Front & Back	(4)	¾" x 4½" x 18½"	Cherry
Drawer Bottom	(2)	¼" x 15¾" x 17½"	Cherry
Drawer Assembly			
(F) Top**		¾" x 17½" x 41¼"	Cherry
(G) Riser	(3)	¾" x 6¾" x 16¼"	Cherry
(H) Back		¼" x 6¼" x 40¾"	Cherry Plywood
(I) Bottom		¾" x 16½" x 39¼"	Cherry

** Glue up hardwood panels with dowel, biscuit or edge joints as shown in chapter five.

Leg
DIMENSIONS

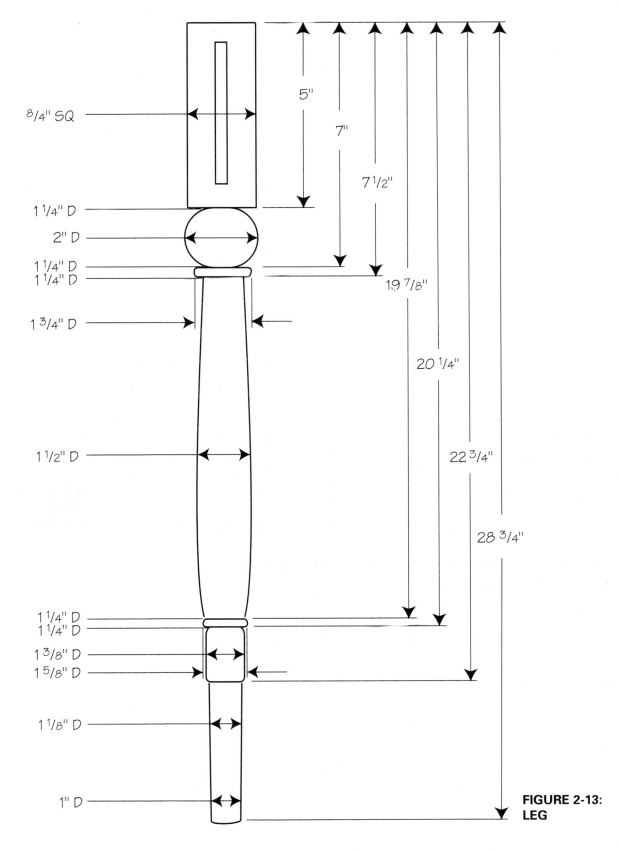

8/4" SQ

1 1/4" D

2" D

1 1/4" D
1 1/4" D

1 3/4" D

1 1/2" D

1 1/4" D
1 1/4" D

1 3/8" D

1 5/8" D

1 1/8" D

1" D

5"

7"

7 1/2"

19 7/8"

20 1/4"

22 3/4"

28 3/4"

FIGURE 2-13:
LEG

Contemporary-Style Secretary

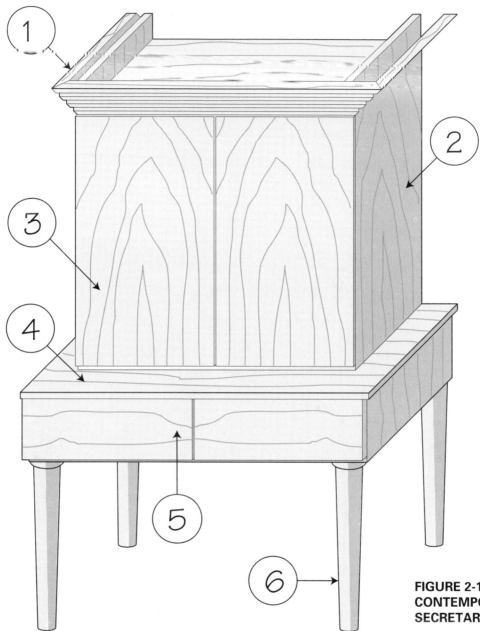

FIGURE 2-14:
CONTEMPORARY-STYLE
SECRETARY

SUBASSEMBLY LIST—CONTEMPORARY-STYLE SECRETARY

No.	Subassembly	Refer to
1	Pediment	Building sequence on page 51.
2	Upper Carcass	Building sequence on page 74.
3	Contemporary Doors	Building sequence in chapter 6.
4	Drawer Assembly	Building sequence on page 71, exploded drawings on page 47.
5	Drawer	Building sequence in chapter 7.
6	Leg	Exploded drawings on page 48.

Drawer Assembly
DIMENSIONS

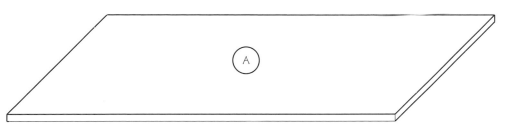

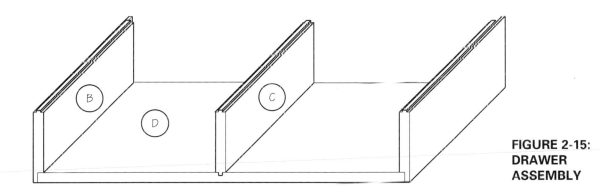

FIGURE 2-15:
DRAWER
ASSEMBLY

CUTTING LIST—CONTEMPORARY-STYLE SECRETARY

Pediment

Pediment Molding*		¾" x 3" x 96"	Cherry

Upper Carcass**

Carcass Side	(2)	¾" x 15½" x 40½"	Cherry Plywood
Top & Bottom	(2)	¾" x 15½" x 38¼"	Cherry Plywood

Contemporary-Style Door

Door**	(2)	¾" x 18½" x 36½"	Cherry Plywood

Drawer Assembly

(A) Top***		¾" x 31¼" x 50"	Cherry
(B) Side	(2)	¾" x 6" x 30½"	Cherry
(C) Middle		¾" x 5¼" x 29¾"	Cherry
(D) Bottom***	(2)	¾" x 29½" x 47¼"	Cherry
(E) Back		¾" x 5½" x 47¼"	Cherry Plywood

Drawer

Drawer Side	(4)	½" x 4½" x 15¾"	Cherry
Drawer Front & Back	(4)	¾" x 4½" x 18½"	Cherry
Drawer Bottom	(2)	¼" x 15¾" x 17½"	Cherry

Leg

Leg****	(4)	1¾" x 1¾" x 24"	Cherry

* Trim to size on the miter saw measuring directly from assembled carcass and face frame.

** Add hardwood edging strips of ¼" cherry to hide plywood edge as shown in chapter four.

*** Glue up hardwood panels with dowel, biscuit or edge joints as shown in chapter five.

**** Attach leg to drawer assembly with Leg Mounting Plates, Part No. 893-673 available from Woodworker's Supply.

Leg
DIMENSIONS

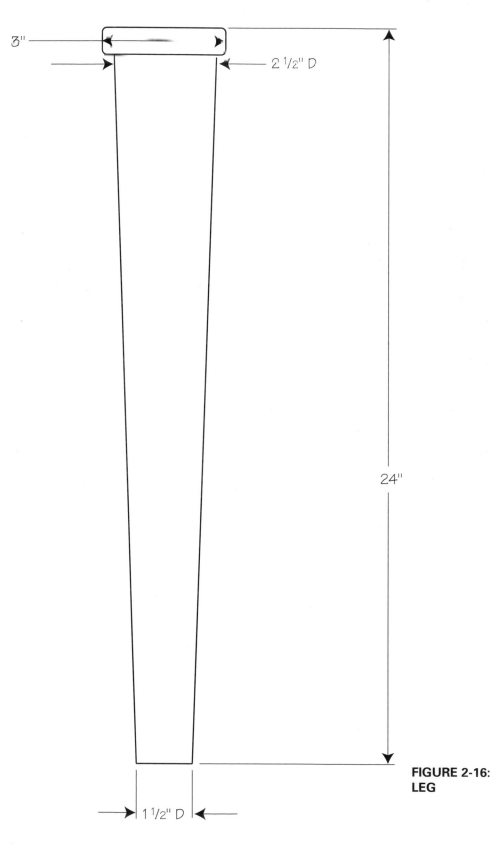

3"

2 1/2" D

24"

1 1/2" D

**FIGURE 2-16:
LEG**

BUILDING FACE FRAMES

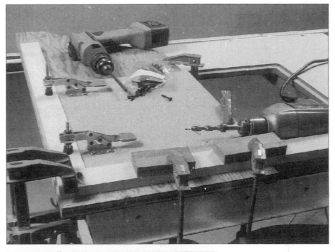

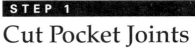

Cut Pocket Joints

Building a solid face frame requires good glue and reinforcement. This jig allows me to position the glued-up workpieces perpendicular to one another, clamp them in position and drill pockets for the hidden pocket screws.

STEP 2

Cut the Biscuit Slots

After the glue has dried and the face frames have been hand planed smooth, mark the location of the biscuits. Cut the slots with a biscuit joiner. I like to cut those joints in just one edge of the carcass and face frame first and then clamp along that edge with the biscuits in place but with no glue. In this fashion, I can hand plane the opposite edge into perfect alignment with the other carcass side before cutting the biscuit joints.

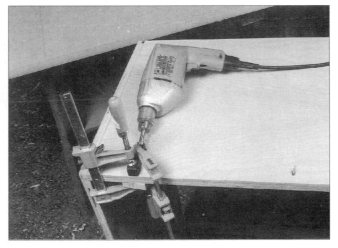

STEP 3

Drill Pockets

Once I've got the biscuit joints cut in both edges, I cut pockets in out-of-sight locations for screwing the face frame to the upper and lower carcass members. You can either drill through the rails and then chisel out the pockets or use the pocket jig to do the same thing.

ASSEMBLING THE SECRETARY

STEP 1

Attach Top to Leg Assembly

After constructing the leg assembly (detailed in chapter five), attach the table to the leg assembly with devices that allow your top to move in response to humidity. Here I've used a tabletop fastener from Woodcraft (#27N10) that fits into a slot you cut with the biscuit joiner.

STEP 2

Attach Drawer Unit to Tabletop

Attach the drawer unit to the tabletop by drilling six holes through the top and screwing into the drawer unit from the underside of the tabletop.

STEP 3

Attach Drawer Unit to Upper Carcass

Once the drawer unit has been fitted to the tabletop, remove the screws holding it to the tabletop and fit it to the bottom of the plywood carcass. Drill and countersink holes for six 1¼" drywall screws from the underside of the drawer unit into the bottom of the carcass. Now screw the drawer unit to the carcass.

STEP 4

Attach Drawer and Upper Carcass to Tabletop

Refit the drawer unit and attached plywood carcass onto the tabletop, and screw the 2" drywall screws home.

BUILDING THE PEDIMENT MOLDINGS

STEP 1

Prepare Molding

Now prepare the moldings by milling an 8' length of ¾" x 4½" oak. After this piece is square and true, rip 45° bevels on both edges and then route these 45° bevels smooth with a 45° beveling bit on the router table. Sand and finish the faces of this pediment molding.

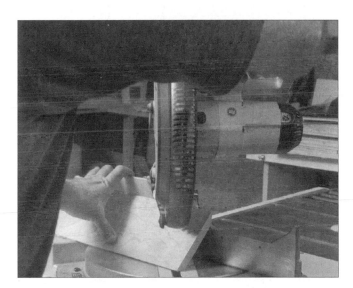

STEP 2

Cut Compound Miters

Beg, borrow or steal some access time on one of those large chop saws you might find in a cabinet shop or at a finish carpenter's job site. You need a saw with at least a 12" blade. Cut the 45° compound miters.

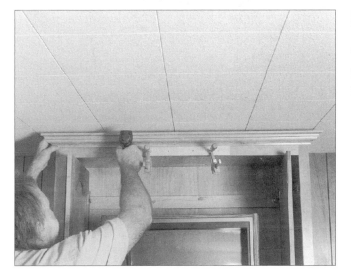

STEP 3

Attach Pediment

Nail the pediment moldings in place, set the nails and fill the holes with an appropriate filler.

MAKING THREE-PIECE ENTERTAINMENT CENTERS

The drawings and building sequence at the end of this chapter detail how to build four different styles of this three-piece entertainment center. If you've decided it is the right size for your room, determine which style will look best in your house. Study the drawings and materials list. After reading chapter ten, figure out how much of what you'll need to complete this project, and order the materials from local suppliers, or order them from some of the suppli-

ers listed in the back of the book. Similarly, study the hardware needed to complete the project, browse through chapter eight and order the hardware from some of the suppliers listed in the back of the book or buy it locally.

After your materials and hardware arrive, begin building. Go first to chapters four and five and plot how you're going to build the needed carcasses for this project. After the plywood carcasses are built,

study the steps in face-frame construction detailed in chapter two on page 49, and attach the face frames to your cabinets. (Face frames are not needed for contemporary-style entertainment centers.)

Now build the drawers and doors, chapters six and seven, and then install the hardware, chapter eight. Finish the components as per chapter nine, and now read the remainder of this chapter to complete your project.

CUTTING LIST—COUNTRY-STYLE THREE-PIECE ENTERTAINMENT CENTER

Pediment

Pediment Molding*		¾" x 3" x 155"	Maple

Upper Carcass

Carcass Side	(2)	¾" x 22¾" x 53"	Birch Plywood
Top & Bottom	(2)	¾" x 22¾" x 42¼"	Birch Plywood
Face-Frame Sides	(2)	¾" x 2" x 53"	Maple
Face-Frame Crosspieces	(2)	¾" x 2" x 39"	Maple

Country-Style Door

Upper Rail	(2)	¾" x 6" x 13½"	Maple
Stile	(4)	¾" x 3" x 41⅛"	Maple
Lower Rail	(2)	¾" x 3½" x 13½"	Maple
Panel	(2)	¾" x 13½" x 35¼"	Maple

Counter and Base

Edging*		¼" x 5" x 155"	Maple
Center Panel	(2)	¼" x 14¾" x 97"	Medium-Density Fiberboard (MDF)

Lower Carcass

Side Rail	(4)	¾" x ½" x 18"	Maple
Carcass Stile	(4)	¾" x 4" x 30"	Maple
Side Panel	(2)	¾" x 18" x 24"	Maple
Rear Stile	(2)	¾" x 3½" x 41¾"	Maple
Rear Panel		¼" x 24" x 41¾"	Birch Plywood
Side Slide Support	(4)	⅝" x 2" x 22"	Maple
Lower Side Slide Support	(2)	⅝" x 3½" x 17"	Maple
Front Center Stiles	(3)	1⅛" x 1⅛" x 9¼"	Maple
Center Slide Support	(3)	1⅛" x 1⅛" x 22"	Maple
Front Rail	(4)	1⅛" x 1⅛" x 41¾"	Maple
Rear Center Stile		1⅛" x 1⅛" x 30"	Maple

Drawer

Drawer Front	(6)	¾" x 7⅞" x 46"	Maple
Drawer Front & Back	(12)	½" x 7⅞" x 45"	Maple
Drawer Side	(12)	½" x 7⅞" x 23½"	Maple
Drawer Bottom	(6)	¼" x 24" x 45½"	Maple

Foot

Foot**	(6)	⅞" x 5" x 10½"	Maple

Side Upper Carcass

Carcass Side	(4)	⅞" x 14½" x 46"	Birch Plywood
Top & Bottom	(4)	¾" x 14½" x 28"	Birch Plywood
Face-Frame Sides	(4)	¾" x 2" x 46"	Maple
Face-Frame Crosspieces	(4)	¾" x 2" x 25"	Maple

Side Lower Carcass

Carcass Side	(4)	¾" x 18" x 30"	Birch Plywood
Top & Bottom	(4)	¾" x 18" x 30¾"	Birch Plywood
Face-Frame Sides	(4)	¾" x 2" x 30"	Maple
Face-Frame Crosspieces	(4)	¾" x 2" x 26¾"	Maple

Door for Lower Carcass

Rail	(8)	¾" x 3" x 8¾"	Maple
Stile	(8)	¾" x 3" x 26¼"	Maple
Panel	(4)	¾" x 9¾" x 22⅜"	Maple

* Miter molding to size taking measurements directly from completed carcass.

** Shape enough extra foot material to make long feet for ends of side unit base.

Country-Style Three-Piece Entertainment Center

SUBASSEMBLY LIST—COUNTRY-STYLE THREE-PIECE ENTERTAINMENT CENTER

No.	Subassembly	Refer to
1	Pediment	Exploded drawings on page 62.
2	Upper Carcass and Face Frame	Exploded drawings on page 63.
3	Country-Style Doors	Exploded drawings on page 62.
4	Counter and Base	Exploded drawings on page 64.
5	Lower Carcass	Exploded drawings on page 65.
6	Drawer	Exploded drawings on page 64.
7	Country-Style Foot	Exploded drawings on page 17.
8	Upper Side Carcass	Exploded drawings on page 66.
9	Lower Side Carcass	Exploded drawings on page 67.
10	Small Door	Exploded drawings on page 62.

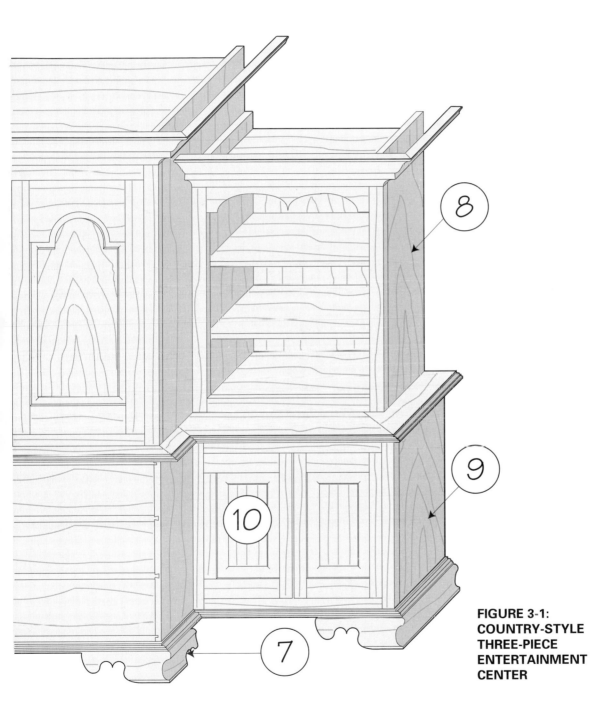

**FIGURE 3-1:
COUNTRY-STYLE
THREE-PIECE
ENTERTAINMENT
CENTER**

Mission-Style Three-Piece Entertainment Center

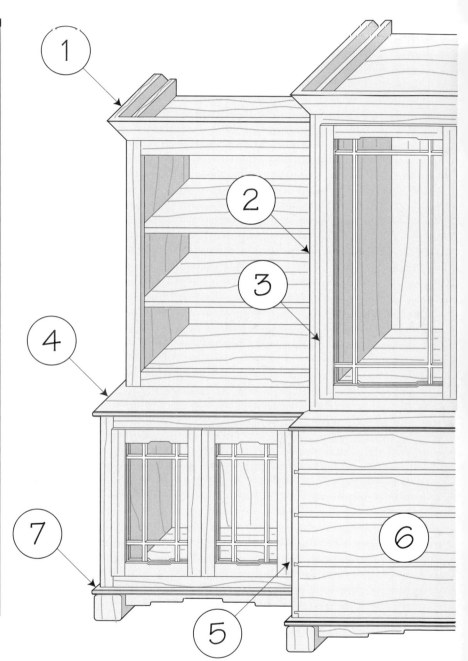

SUBASSEMBLY LIST—MISSION-STYLE THREE-PIECE ENTERTAINMENT CENTER

No.	Subassembly	Refer to
1	Pediment	Exploded drawings on page 62.
2	Upper Carcass and Face Frame	Exploded drawings on page 63.
3	Mission-Style Doors	Exploded drawings on page 62.
4	Counter	Exploded drawings on page 64.
5	Lower Carcass	Exploded drawings on page 65.
6	Drawer	Exploded drawings on page 64.
7	Mission-Style Base	Exploded drawings on page 66.
8	Upper Side Carcass	Exploded drawings on page 66.
9	Lower Side Carcass	Exploded drawings on page 67.
10	Small Door	Exploded drawings on page 62.

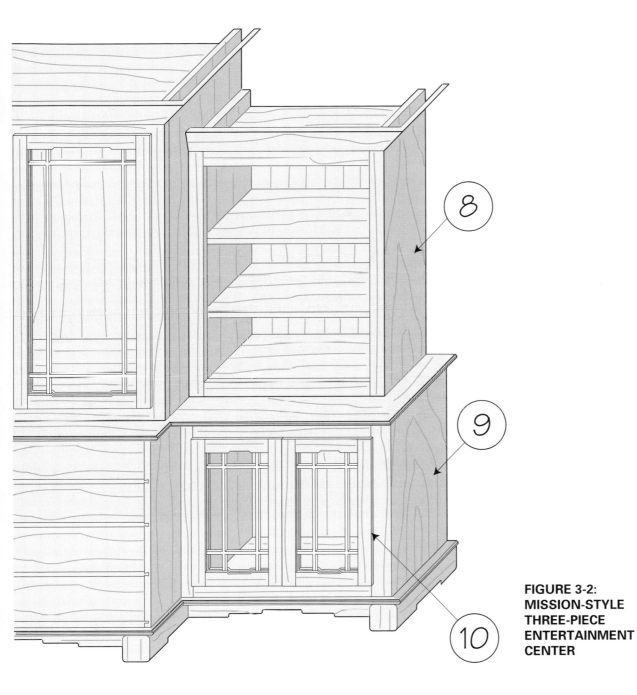

**FIGURE 3-2:
MISSION-STYLE
THREE-PIECE
ENTERTAINMENT
CENTER**

CUTTING LIST—MISSION-STYLE THREE-PIECE ENTERTAINMENT CENTER

Pediment			
Pediment Molding		¾" x 5" x 155"	Oak
Upper Carcass			
Carcass Side	(2)	¾" x 22¾" x 53"	Oak Plywood
Top & Bottom	(2)	¾" x 22¾" x 42¼"	Oak Plywood
Face-Frame Sides	(2)	¾" x 2" x 53"	Oak
Face-Frame Crosspieces	(2)	¾" x 2" x 39¾"	Oak
Mission-Style Door			
Upper & Lower Rail	(4)	¾" x 4" x 14½"	Oak
Stile	(4)	¾" x 25" x 41⅞"	Oak
Glass Panel	(2)	¾" x 14¼" x 34⅞"	Leaded or Etched Glass
Counter			
Center Panel	(2)	¾" x 22" x 37"	Medium-Density Fiberboard (MDF)
Edging*	(2)	¾" x 5" x 155"	Oak
Lower Carcass			
Side	(2)	¾" x 24" x 30"	Oak Plywood
Rear Panel		¼" x 30" x 44"	Oak Plywood
Crosspiece	(4)	¾" x 4" x 4½"	Oak
Divider	(6)	¾" x 1½" x 44½"	Oak
Drawer			
Drawer Front	(4)	¾" x 7⅛" x 42½"	Oak
Drawer Back	(4)	½" x 6⅞" x 4½"	Oak
Drawer Side	(8)	½" x 6⅞" x 20"	Oak
Drawer Bottom	(4)	¼" x 19½" x 42"	Oak
Mission-Style Base			
Feet	(4)	12/12" x 12/12" x 24"	Oak
Center Crosspiece		¾" x 2" x 39"	Oak
Side Crosspiece	(2)	¾" x 2" x 27"	Oak
Side Upper Carcass			
Carcass Side	(4)	¾" x 14½" x 46"	Oak Plywood
Top & Bottom	(4)	¾" x 14½" x 28"	Oak Plywood
Face-Frame Sides	(4)	¾" x 2" x 46"	Oak
Face-Frame Crosspieces	(4)	¾" x 2" x 25"	Oak
Side Lower Carcass			
Carcass Side	(4)	¾" x 18" x 30"	Oak Plywood
Top & Bottom	(4)	¾" x 18" x 30¾"	Oak Plywood
Face-Frame Sides	(4)	¾" x 2" x 30"	Oak
Face-Frame Crosspieces	(4)	¾" x 2" x 26¾"	Oak
Door for Lower Carcass			
Rail	(8)	¾" x 3" x ¾"	Oak
Stile	(8)	¾" x 3" x 26¼"	Oak
Panel	(4)	¾" x 9¾" x 22⅜"	Oak

* Miter molding, edging to size taking measurements directly from completed carcass.

CUTTING LIST—SHAKER-STYLE THREE-PIECE ENTERTAINMENT CENTER

Pediment			
Pediment Molding*		¾" x 3" x 155"	Cherry
Upper Carcass			
(A) Carcass Side	(2)	¾" x 22¾" x 53"	Cherry Plywood
(B) Top & Bottom	(2)	¾" x 22¾" x 42¼"	Cherry Plywood
(C) Face-Frame Crosspieces	(2)	¾" x 2" x 39⅜"	Cherry
(D) Face-Frame Sides	(2)	¾" x 2" x 53"	Cherry
Shaker-Style Door			
(E) Upper & Lower Rail	(4)	¾" x 3" x 14¾"	Cherry
(F) Stile	(4)	¾" x 3" x 46⅝"	Cherry
(G) Panel	(2)	¼" x 14¾" x 39¾"	Cherry Plywood
Counter			
(H) Center Panel		¾" x 22" x 97"	Medium-Density Fiberboard (MDF)
(I) Edging*		¾" x 5" x 155"	Cherry
Lower Carcass			
(J) Side	(2)	¾" x 24" x 30"	Cherry Plywood
(K) Crosspiece	(4)	¾" x 4" x 44½"	Cherry
(L) Divider	(8)	¾" x 1½" x 44½"	Cherry
(M) Rear Panel		¼" x 30" x 44"	Cherry Plywood
(N) Screw Block	(10)	¾" x 1½" x 1½"	Cherry
Drawer			
(O) Drawer Front & Back	(2)	¾" x 7⅛" x 42½"	Cherry
(O) Drawer Front & Back	(2)	¾" x 6⅛" x 4½"	Cherry
(O) Drawer Front & Back	(2)	¾" x 5⅛" x 4½"	Cherry
(O) Drawer Front & Back	(2)	¾" x 4⅛" x 42½"	Cherry
(O) Drawer Front & Back	(2)	¾" x 3⅛" x 4 ½"	Cherry
(P) Drawer Bottom	(5)	¼" x 19½" x 42"	Cherry
(Q) Drawer Side	(2)	½" x 7⅛" x 20"	Cherry
(Q) Drawer Side	(2)	½" x 6⅛" x 20"	Cherry
(Q) Drawer Side	(2)	½" x 5⅛" x 20"	Cherry
(Q) Drawer Side	(2)	½" x 4⅛" x 20"	Cherry
(Q) Drawer Side	(2)	½" x 3⅛" x 20"	Cherry
Base and feet			
(R) Back		⁸⁄₄" x 5" x 105"	Cherry
(S) Center Front		⁸⁄₄" x 5" x 46¾"	Cherry
(T) Side Front	(2)	⁸⁄₄" x 5" x 33"	Cherry
(U) Sides	(2)	⁸⁄₄" x 5" x 16½"	Cherry
(V) Center Sides	(2)	⁸⁄₄" x 5" x 25¾"	Cherry
(W) Gusset	(8)	¾" x 10" x 10"	Cherry Plywood
Side Upper Carcass			
(W) Carcass Side	(4)	¾" x 14½" x 46"	Cherry Plywood
(X) Top & Bottom	(4)	¾" x 14½" x 28"	Cherry Plywood
(Y) Face-Frame Sides	(4)	¾" x 2" x 46"	Cherry
(Z) Face-Frame Crosspieces	(4)	¾" x 2" x 25"	Cherry
Side Lower Carcass			
(W) Carcass Side	(4)	¾" x 18" x 30"	Cherry Plywood
(X) Top & Bottom	(4)	¾" x 18" x 30¾"	Cherry Plywood
(Y) Face-Frame Sides	(4)	¾" x 2" x 30"	Cherry
(Z) Face-Frame Crosspieces	(4)	¾" x 2" x 26¾"	Cherry
Door for Lower Carcass			
Rail	(8)	¾" x 3" x 8¾"	Cherry
Stile	(8)	¾" x 3" x 26¼"	Cherry
Panel	(4)	¾" x 9¾" x 22⅜"	Cherry

* Miter molding, edging to size taking measurements directly from completed carcass.

Shaker-Style Three-Piece Entertainment Center

No.	Subassembly	Refer to
	SUBASSEMBLY LIST—SHAKER-STYLE THREE-PIECE ENTERTAINMENT CENTER	
1	Pediment	Exploded drawings on page 62.
2	Upper Carcass and Face Frame	Exploded drawings on page 63.
3	Shaker-Style Doors	Exploded drawings on page 62.
4	Counter	Exploded drawings on page 64.
5	Lower Carcass	Exploded drawings on page 65.
6	Drawer	Exploded drawings on page 64.
7	Shaker Base	Exploded drawings on page 66.
8	Upper Side Carcass	Exploded drawings on page 66.
9	Lower Side Carcass	Exploded drawings on page 67.
10	Small Door	Exploded drawings on page 62.

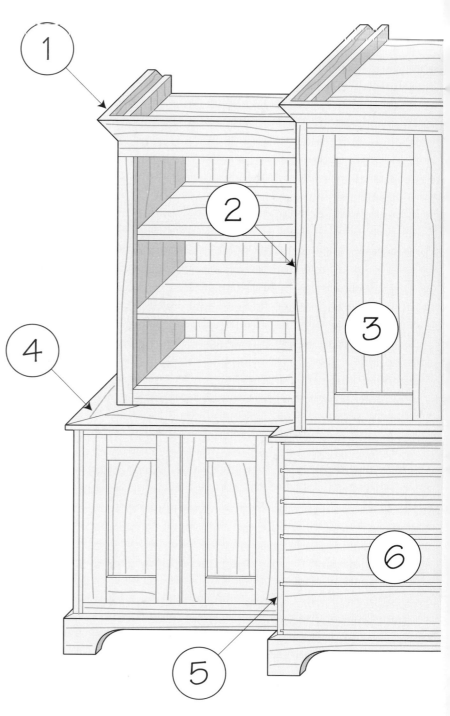

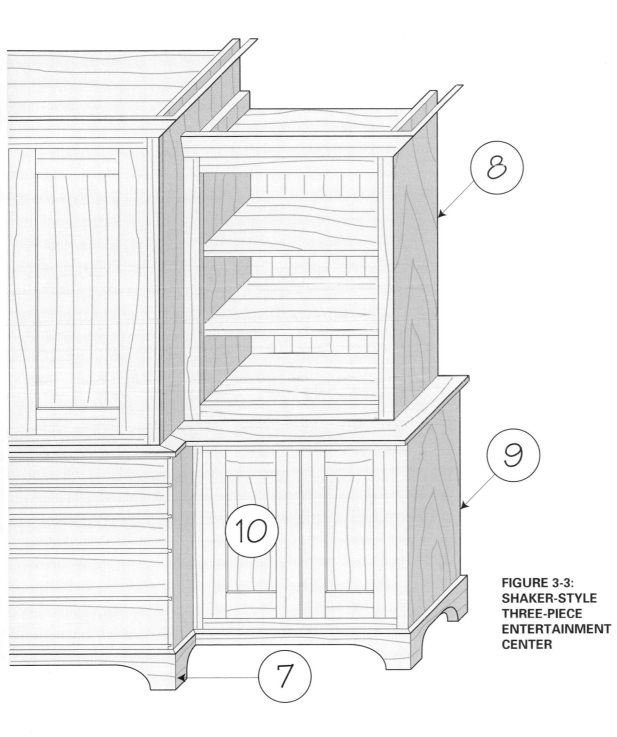

**FIGURE 3-3:
SHAKER-STYLE
THREE-PIECE
ENTERTAINMENT
CENTER**

Pediment and Door
DIMENSIONS

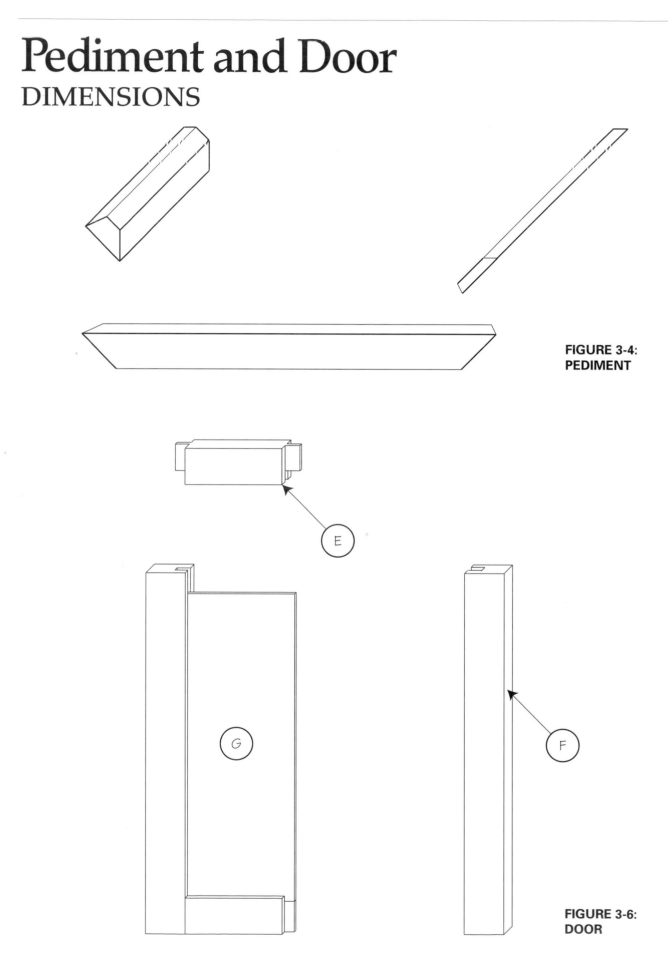

**FIGURE 3-4:
PEDIMENT**

**FIGURE 3-6:
DOOR**

Upper Carcass
DIMENSIONS

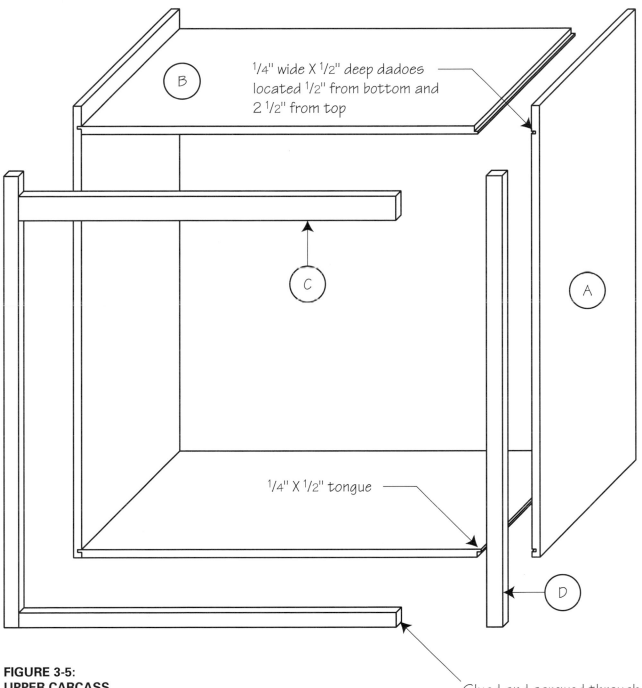

1/4" wide X 1/2" deep dadoes located 1/2" from bottom and 2 1/2" from top

Ⓑ

Ⓒ

Ⓐ

1/4" X 1/2" tongue

Ⓓ

FIGURE 3-5:
UPPER CARCASS
AND FACE FRAME

Glued and screwed through pocket joints cut on back side of face frame.

Counter, Lower Carcass and Drawer

DIMENSIONS

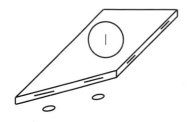

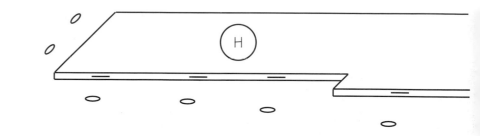

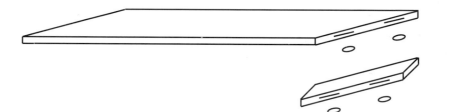

FIGURE 3-7:
COUNTER

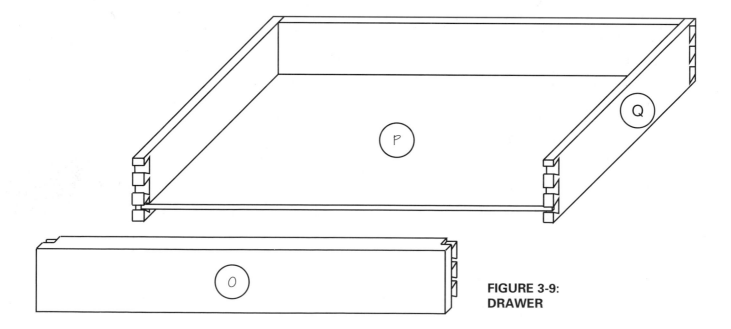

FIGURE 3-9:
DRAWER

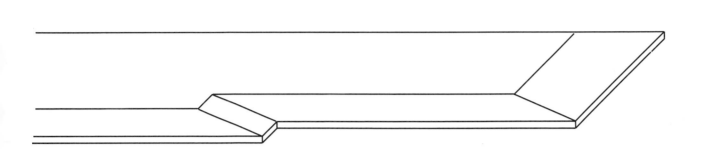

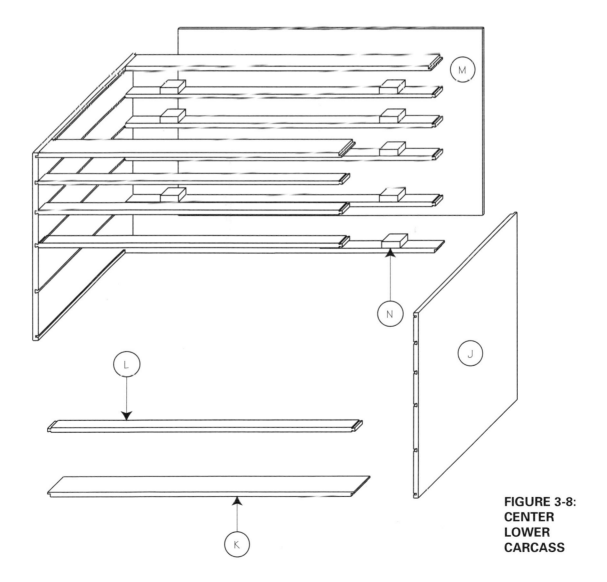

**FIGURE 3-8:
CENTER
LOWER
CARCASS**

Base and Side Unit Upper and Lower Carcass
DIMENSIONS

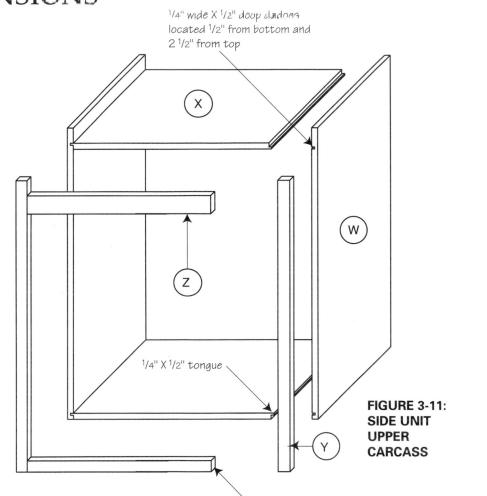

¹/4" wide X ¹/2" deep dadoes located ¹/2" from bottom and 2 ¹/2" from top

X

W

Z

¹/4" X ¹/2" tongue

Y

**FIGURE 3-11:
SIDE UNIT
UPPER
CARCASS**

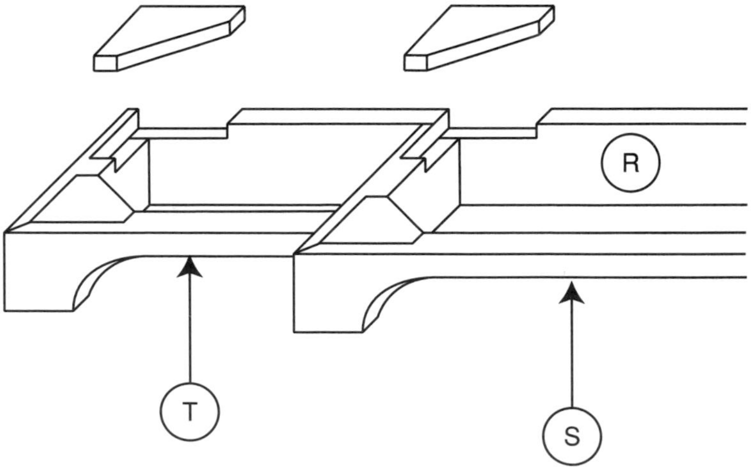

Glued and screwed through pocket joints cut on back side of face frame.

R

T

S

**FIGURE 3-10:
BASE ASSEMBLY**

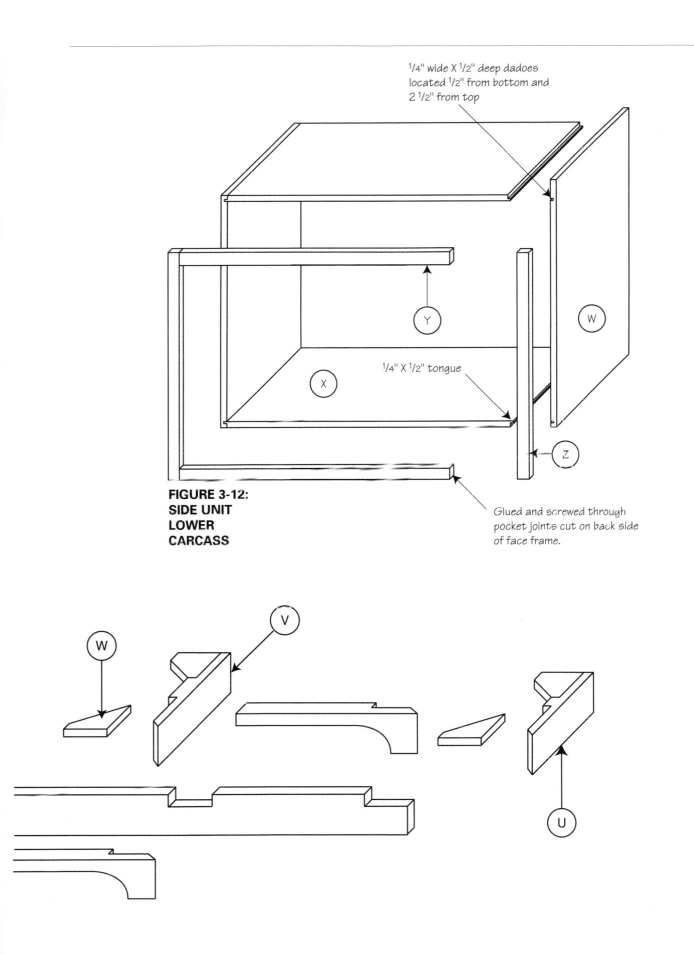

¹/4" wide X ¹/2" deep dadoes located ¹/2" from bottom and 2 ¹/2" from top

¹/4" X ¹/2" tongue

FIGURE 3-12: SIDE UNIT LOWER CARCASS

Glued and screwed through pocket joints cut on back side of face frame.

Contemporary-Style Three-Piece Entertainment Center

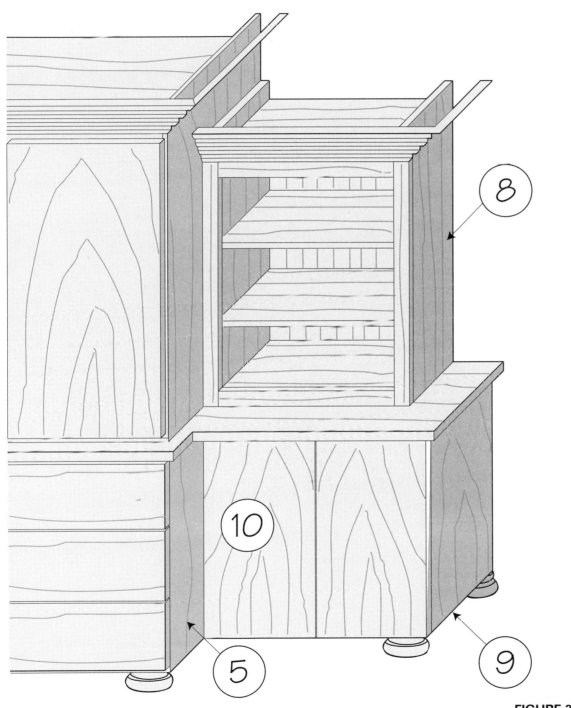

**FIGURE 3-13:
CONTEMPORARY-
STYLE THREE-PIECE
ENTERTAINMENT
CENTER**

CUTTING LIST—CONTEMPORARY-STYLE THREE-PIECE ENTERTAINMENT CENTER

Pediment

Pediment Molding*		¾" x 5" x 155"	Maple

Upper Carcass

Carcass Side	(2)	¾" x 22¾" x 53"	Maple Plywood
Top & Bottom	(2)	¾" x 22¾" x 43¼"	Maple Plywood

Contemporary-Style Door

Door	(2)	¾" x 2¼" x 49¼"	Maple Plywood**

Counter

Center Panel		¾" x 22" x 97"	Medium-Density Fiberboard (MDF)
Edging*		¾" x 5" x 155"	Maple

Lower Carcass

Side	(2)	¾" x 24" x 30"	Maple Plywood
Rear Panel		¼" x 30" x 43¼"	Maple Plywood
Crosspiece	(4)	¾" x 4" x 43¼"	Maple
Center Divider		¾" x 24" x 34"	Maple Plywood

Drawer

Drawer Front	(6)	¾" x 10" x 21¼"	Maple
Drawer Front & Back	(12)	½" x 9" x 20⅜"	Poplar
Drawer Side	(8)	½" x 9" x 20"	Poplar
Drawer Bottom	(4)	¼" x 19½" x 19⅞"	Birch Plywood

Foot

Small Foot	(8)	8½" Dia disk of ¾"	Maple

Large Foot	(8)	9½" Dia Disk of ¾"	Maple

Side Upper Carcass

Carcass Side	(4)	¾" x 14½" x 46"	Birch Plywood
Top & Bottom	(4)	¾" x 14½" x 28"	Birch Plywood
Face-Frame Sides	(4)	¾" x 2" x 46"	Maple
Face-Frame Crosspieces	(4)	¾" x 2" x 25"	Maple

Side Lower Carcass

Carcass Side	(4)	¾" x 18" x 30"	Birch Plywood
Top & Bottom	(4)	¾" x 18" x 30¾"	Birch Plywood
Face-Frame Sides	(4)	¾" x 2" x 30"	Maple
Face-Frame Crosspieces	(4)	¾" x 2" x 26¾"	Maple

Door for Lower Carcass

Door	(2)	¾" x 15⅜" x 29¼"	Maple Plywood

* Pediment molding profile cut on the router table with a 45° bevel bit mounted in the router. Miter molding, edging to size taking measurements directly from the upper carcasses.

** Upper and lower carcass and doors are edged with hardwood strips as shown in chapter four.

COMPLETING THE DRAWER UNIT

STEP 1

Cut Dovetail Tenons

Cut the dovetail tenons on the ends of the drawer dividers to fit the dovetail mortises you cut when you built the plywood cabinet carcasses in chapter four. I use an accessory I built for my router table.

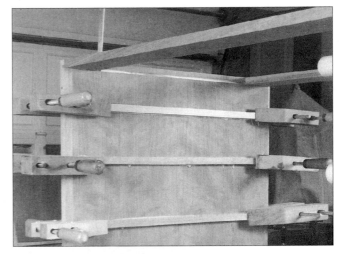

STEP 2

Cut Tongues

Cut tongues on 1¼"-wide pieces of cherry to fit the dadoes you cut earlier. I used a table-mounted router and a ¼" straight bit. Glue and clamp these rails in place, leaving a 1¼" space for the dovetailed pieces.

STEP 3

Make and Install Drawer Stops

Once the front and rear crosspieces are glued in place, screw 1¼" drywall screws into one edge of each of ten 1¼" square blocks of ¾" cherry stock. Then glue two of the stop blocks about three inches from each end of the chest with the screwhead facing the back of the drawers. These screws act as adjustable drawer stops so your drawer fronts will always be aligned with the front of the chest.

STEP 4

Trim Drawers to Ideal Fit

To fit the drawer fronts perfectly, establish the ideal fit of the drawer (about ¹⁄₁₆" gap all around), and then wedge each drawer into ideal position, using the drywall screws in the blocks at the back of each drawer to position the drawer in the correct position. Finally, when the drawer is positioned in the optimum position and locked in place with the wedges, cut off the wedges flush with the drawer front, and belt sand the drawers, crosspieces and sides of the cabinet into perfect alignment.

ASSEMBLING THE CARCASS

STEP 1

Build the Base and Counter

Cut the miters for the Shaker-style cabinet base on the mitering sled shown in the photo above and the photo sequence in chapter one on page 30.

STEP 2

Square Up the Panel

It's difficult to square up a big panel. I routed this big panel square with a straight-edged pattern bit riding against a straightedge.

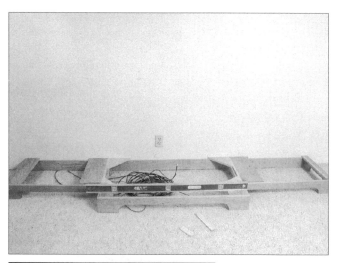

STEP 3

Level the Base

Make sure you pull the baseboard molding and cut the recess for the tack strip under the carpet into the rear feet. Here I am checking for level during the installation of the base for the three-piece Shaker-style entertainment center. Once level, locate the studs with a stud finder, and then mark their locations. Finally, screw the back rail of the base to the wall with 3" drywall screws. (Don't forget to have electrical, communications, video and stereo cables pulled and in position prior to beginning this installation.)

STEP 4

Level the Lower Cabinets

Check for level for each of the base cabinets, too, and then attach each component to the base with 1¼" drywall screws in unseen places. I drill and countersink each screw location even though drywall screws make their own holes.

Cut Holes for Wiring and Ventilation

To cut holes for cables, I cut a 2⅜"-diameter hole in a piece of ½" MDF with a hole saw in the drill press and then use that template to locate and rout perfect replicas anywhere I need them. I use a brace of Porter Cable routers, one a plunge router and the other a fixed-base router. I mount a template guide in the plunge router base and a ½" spiral cut mortising bit to rough-cut the hole to within ⅛" of the final size. Then I cut the hole to exact size with a straight-edged pattern bit in the fixed-base router.

Cut Wood for Knobs

I used some fancy brass knobs that let you customize your project by gluing in matching or contrasting woods in the knob and then turning it to size and shape. These knobs are available from Woodcraft (part number 123551). I used an epoxy glue to attach the wood to the brass. Woodcraft also has a tiny mandrel (part number 111188) that helps you mount the knob in your lathe or drill press. Incidentally, I used maple as a contrasting wood. I have already bored the 1" plugs for the knobs in this piece of maple using a 1" tenoner (you could also use a plug cutter). I am holding the plugs securely in place with a piece of duct tape across the outer face of the board. I resawed the plugs free by raising the blade about an inch per pass.

Glue Discs to Brass Knobs

Once the plugs are free, just peel back the duct tape and voila, perfect 1" discs. Epoxy the discs to the brass knobs, turn them on the lathe or drill press and attach to the doors.

CHAPTER FOUR

BUILDING PLYWOOD CABINET CARCASSES

The basic building block of the cabinetmaking universe is the plywood carcass. Simply stated, a carcass is a cube formed of plywood, perfectly square and very strong. The ubiquitous plywood cabinet carcass is quick to make, is simply joined and offers endless possible combinations for stacking, hanging and attaching to walls, ceilings, floors and other carcasses.

PREPARING SQUARE STOCK

The key to successful carcasses is paying rigorous attention to the basic premise of woodworking: square stock. You must be able to produce flawless 90° angles and smooth, crisp edges in sheets of plywood—no mean feat when you consider they are 4' wide and 8' long and they weigh some 50 to 60 pounds. I maintain a two-stage stock preparation routine that lets me hide my inconsistencies: I first make rough cuts to break down these big plywood sheets into the needed parts while leaving enough waste for me to trim to size with highly accurate final cuts.

BREAK DOWN THE PLYWOOD SHEETS

STEP 1

Plan Your Cuts

The first step in building a carcass is cutting a sheet of plywood into the parts you need. Using the letters assigned to each part on the materials lists and the exploded drawings for the design, I sketch in the cut lines for each of the parts and write the letter of the part on that sketch. Remember to pay close attention to the desired grain direction of each part.

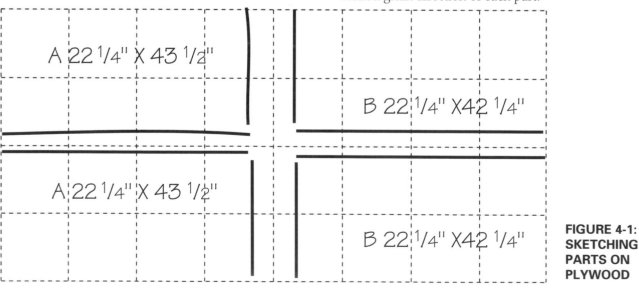

A 22 1/4" X 43 1/2"

B 22 1/4" X 42 1/4"

A 22 1/4" X 43 1/2"

B 22 1/4" X 42 1/4"

FIGURE 4-1: SKETCHING PARTS ON PLYWOOD

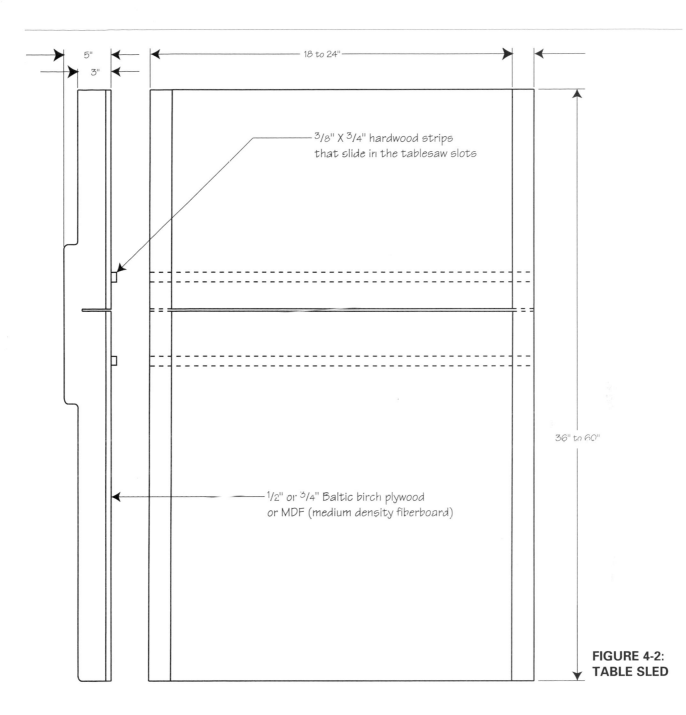

5"

3"

18 to 24"

3/8" X 3/4" hardwood strips
that slide in the tablesaw slots

36" to 60"

1/2" or 3/4" Baltic birch plywood
or MDF (medium density fiberboard)

**FIGURE 4-2:
TABLE SLED**

Rough-Cut the Pieces

First, I stack all of my plywood at the same height and adjacent to the outfeed table of my table saw. I pull the plywood onto the table saw and then slide it back to rest on a support placed about seven feet behind the table saw. In this fashion I avoid having to lift the plywood, and consequently, I avoid smashing edges and corners. Once the workpiece is positioned ready for the cut, I adjust the fence to the right width, raise the saw blade so the teeth project no more than 1/8" above the workpiece, turn on the saw and begin the cut. Note in the

photo page 74, that I am positioned at the left rear corner of the plywood sheet. I concentrate on keeping the plywood edge riding smoothly against the fence. As I approach the midpoint of the plywood sheet, I move more toward the middle of the workpiece, directly behind the table saw.

You next need to crosscut the long plywood panels into the right lengths. Once I've rough-cut a part, I write the letter of the part on the two ends of the workpiece so I don't get confused later. I use the table saw sled to get the kind of safe, highly accurate cut I want to make. The drawing above shows how I build my table saw sled for crosscutting big plywood panels.

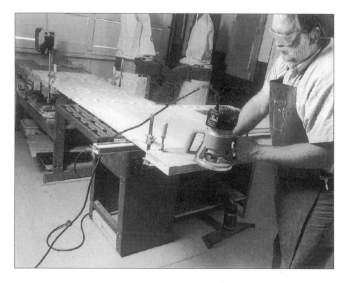

Cutting Large Pieces

Occasionally, you'll have to crosscut a piece that's too big for your sled. In this case I crosscut with one square end riding against the fence, a more dangerous proposition, but one I can manage by paying extra attention to maintaining firm contact between the workpiece and the fence. Crosscutting in this fashion follows whatever angle rides against the fence, so you must make sure that end is exactly square to the long edge of the plywood. Trim the end square with a router and pattern bit riding against a straightedge clamped to the workpiece as shown in the photo at left.

STEP 3

Trim to Final Size

Trimming to final size is where I really get fussy. I put my best blade on the table saw, hone or change my jointer blades and check all of my fences for squareness. I begin at the jointer and joint a smooth, true edge on one long edge of each workpiece, identifying that edge with a slashed pencil line across it. After I've worked my way through the pile of rough-cut plywood parts, I carefully rip each piece to final dimension plus $\frac{1}{16}$" and then joint that edge to final size. Now I'll bring out the table saw sled again and crosscut a true 90° end on each piece, marking it with a slashed pencil line. Finally, I crosscut the opposite end square and to size, using stop blocks clamped to the sled's rail or to the table saw's auxiliary table to ensure like parts are exactly the same length. As you cut off the ends, re-mark the letter identifying each piece.

EDGING PLYWOOD

Most of the exposed edges of the plywood are covered by face frames and don't need edging, but the contemporary designs and the center lower cabinet of the three-piece Shaker-style entertainment center must be edged prior to assembly. You could argue that the rear edges of the plywood are not seen and consequently don't need to be edged, but I can't sleep nights unless I do a thorough job of edging, and that includes these unseen areas. Regardless of where you fall in the debate about fixing unseen blemishes, you'll need to apply edging to the plywood, even if it's only for shelving.

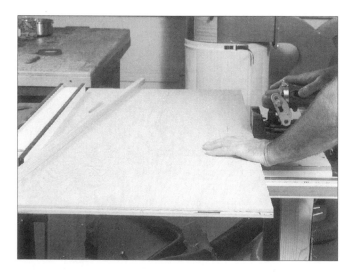

Biscuit-Joined Edges

For biscuit-joined edging, rip and joint a number of lengths of 4/4 hardwood in the same species as your plywood. Try to match grain as much as possible, but avoid curly or highly figured wood as it is difficult to hand plane. Make sure the edging is slightly thicker than your plywood. Position the edging against the plywood edge where you want it to go, and draw lines across the edging and plywood with a square and pencil to identify where the biscuits will be placed. I like to insert a biscuit about every 12 inches. Now plunge the biscuit joiner blade in at each pencil mark on the plywood and edging.

Nailed Edging

I prefer to deal with the edging destined to be facing the wall by just gluing and nailing ¼"-wide hardwood strips to the plywood as shown in the photo at left. Set the nails below the surface of the wood.

Edge Finishing

With both biscuit-joined and nailed edging, once the glue has dried, hand plane the edging flush with the plywood's surface with a sharp block plane canted at a 45° angle. If you find you are gouging the plywood's veneer, resharpen your plane iron or clamp a straight-edge along the workpiece so the plane's blade can only cut the edging. Trim the edging to exact size on the radial arm saw or table saw using the jig shown in the drawing below.

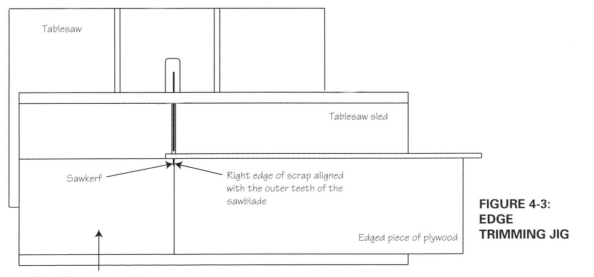

Tablesaw

Tablesaw sled

Sawkerf

Right edge of scrap aligned with the outer teeth of the sawblade

Edged piece of plywood

**FIGURE 4-3:
EDGE
TRIMMING JIG**

Piece of scrap same or less width as the plywood without the edging, screwed to MDF

CARCASS JOINERY

Joinery for plywood cabinet carcasses is simple, straightforward and relatively easy to cut. For the most part, it consists of butt joints, rabbets and dadoes, but the Shaker-style entertainment center requires some simple-to-make sliding dovetails.

TONGUE-AND-DADO JOINTS

STEP 1
Score the Edges

Probably the most difficult part of cutting joinery in plywood is figuring out how to avoid splitting and chipping the veneer. You can avoid such problems by using a utility knife to score lines where the joint will occur.

You make the first half of the tongue-and-dado joint just like a dado: You simply plough a dado with an edge riding against the fence.

STEP 2
Cut the Dadoes

You could use the radial arm saw or rout dadoes with a router mounted in a router table or a portable router. For accuracy and convenience, I prefer to use a stack dado head mounted on the table saw arbor. The dado is just ¼" wide, and it is located ¾" from the edge of the workpiece. The challenge now is to rout a tongue that just slips into the dado. I prefer to do this on the router table, although you could certainly use the dado head to perform this task.

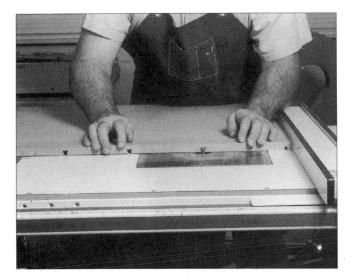

SLIDING DOVETAILS

STEP 1

Score the Edges

The first step in cutting the sliding dovetails for the lower center cabinet carcass for the three-piece Shaker-style entertainment center proceeds just like above, except the sliding dovetails are centered at the dimensions listed on the exploded drawings shown on page 65.

STEP 2

Cut the Dadoes

Once I've ploughed the ¼" rectangular dado all the way across the inside of the carcass sides, I mount a 14° dovetail bit in my router and mount it in turn in my router table. To cut the 1"-long sliding dovetails that carry the drawer rails, I use the same fence settings as used to cut the dadoes. Draw a mark one inch from the center of the router bit on either side of the fence, and use these marks as stopping points for the workpiece. You need to maintain extra vigilance at pressing the workpiece firmly against the fence and down onto the table. A moment's inattention may be disastrous for the workpiece and possibly for you. Remember that the dovetail bit is trapped inside the wood. It will quickly grab the workpiece and throw it unpredictably if you are not rigorous in maintaining control.

FINISHING THE CARCASS

Before you assemble the carcasses, drill the shelf-pin holes with a ¼" brad point bit and a stop collar to prevent you drilling all the way through the workpiece. Either make up a drilling jig as shown in the drawing on page 81, or fork over big bucks to one of the mail-order marketers of woodworking para-phernalia listed in the sources of supply at the back of the book. Sand the inside faces of all of the carcass members through 180-grit, stain and fill the grain of any big pored woods like oak. Apply at least one coat of finish to these interior surfaces, then assemble each carcass. Be careful to control squeeze-out. You want squeeze-out to occur where you can chip it out easily or ignore it altogether. Finish the ¼" plywood backing now too, but don't install these pieces until the project nears completion. You will find this extra access handy for cutting holes for cables or ventila-tion, and it's also much easier to connect the carcasses if you can clamp them together through the back of the cabinets at final assembly.

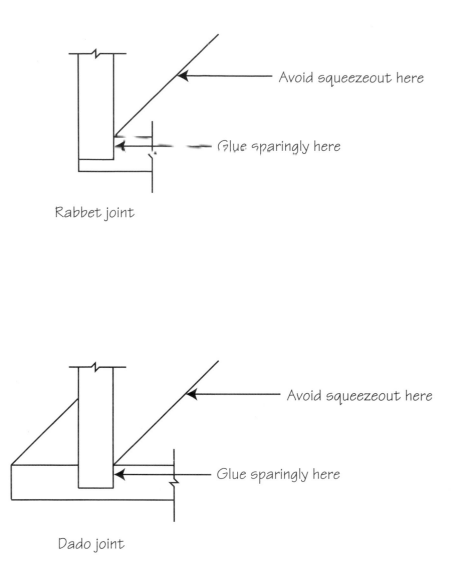

Avoid squeezeout here

Glue sparingly here

Rabbet joint

Avoid squeezeout here

Glue sparingly here

Dado joint

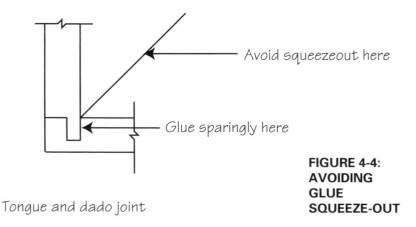

Avoid squeezeout here

Glue sparingly here

FIGURE 4-4: AVOIDING GLUE SQUEEZE-OUT

Tongue and dado joint

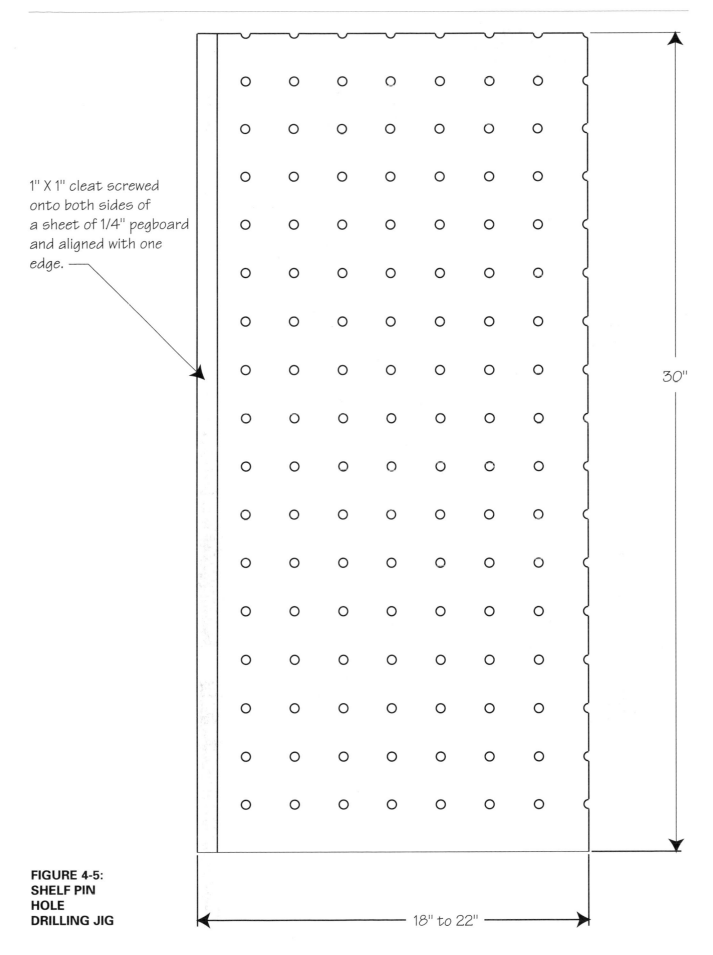

1" X 1" cleat screwed onto both sides of a sheet of 1/4" pegboard and aligned with one edge.

30"

FIGURE 4-5: SHELF PIN HOLE DRILLING JIG

18" to 22"

CHAPTER FIVE

CUSTOMIZING YOUR ENTERTAINMENT CENTER

The aim of this book is to enable you to build an entertainment center without having to attend night classes or buy six new machines. To that end, I designed the three variations of the four styles of entertainment centers you find in the first three chapters. While I'm confident that several, if not all, of these designs will look great in your home, you may find you need to tinker with the design a bit to get it to suit your particular need.

BUILDING SOLID-WOOD CARCASSES

I recommend plywood carcasses for a number of reasons: expense, ease of construction, simplicity and practicality. But I must admit that virtually all first-rate, museum-quality furniture is built of hardwood. You may decide that the look of solid-wood cabinetry is more appropriate for your house.

COUNTERING WOOD MOVEMENT

The chief trick of building solid-wood cabinetry is to allow for the inevitable: the cycle of expansion and contraction across the wood's growth rings. You've got to build so your carcasses can expand and contract without binding, or these pressures will tear your furniture apart. I combat furniture explosions in solid-wood cabinetry by allowing tops, feet, pedestals, etc., to float; which is to say, never screw, glue or nail solid-wood members in more than one place, to allow for cross-grain expansion.

BUILDING PANELS

Building solid-wood panels is one of the basic skills of woodworking, and in order to accomplish it, square stock is essential. To mill stock effectively, you need at least a jointer and a table saw if you are going to biscuit join the panels. You'll need a planer, too, if you are making splined or dowel joints.

Prepare the Stock

Examine the stock to be milled and note any splits, checks, warps or other flaws. You'll want to deal with these in some fashion, either cutting them out, planing them flat or repairing them. Next, reserve the best figure, color and grain for the most noticeable parts.

STEP 2

Mill the Pieces

Rough-cut all pieces to final length plus a couple of inches. Joint a surface and an adjacent edge square on each workpiece. Rip a parallel edge to size plus $\frac{1}{16}$" on the table saw, and then joint that edge smooth and to size. Finally, surface all wood to the same thickness.

STEP 3

Check the Edges

Before you actually begin spreading glue, pay extra attention to the mating edges of the glue joint. You want a slight concavity along the edges as shown in the drawing. To inspect the glue line, clamp a board in your vise, position the second board on top of it and shine a flashlight along the joint line. Hand plane to achieve an optimal fit, and then prepare the edge joints. The following are my three favorite edge joints for large panels.

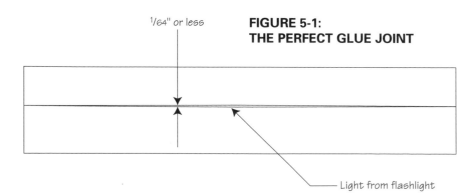

1/64" or less

FIGURE 5-1: THE PERFECT GLUE JOINT

Light from flashlight

MAKING A DOWEL JOINT

STEP 1
Lay Out the Joint

Mark the position where each of the dowels will go while the boards are lying in position. Carry those marks across each board's edge with a square.

STEP 2
Drill the Holes

Position the doweling jig so the hole is aligned with the marks you drew on the edges. Drill the holes with a twist bit or a brad point bit the same diameter as the dowels you're going to use, and use a stop block or a bit of masking tape on the drill bit to mark the right depth.

STEP 3
Assemble the Joint

Glue the edges and dowels, insert the dowels and position the mating board. Pull boards together with clamps.

MAKING SPLINE JOINTS

STEP 1
Cut the Grooves

Cut grooves down the middle of your workpieces along the edges, as shown in the drawing at left. You can rout this groove at the router table with a ¼" or smaller straight cutter mounted in the router. You can also cut it on the table saw in the same position. In either circumstance, I make a pass from each face of the board to assure the groove is centered and clamp a featherboard to the table's surface to ensure a wobble-free pass over the cutter or saw blade.

STEP 2
Make the Spline

After cutting the grooves, it's simply a matter of ripping thin spline material to fit the groove.

STEP 3
Assemble the Joint

Glue the edges, the groove and the spline. Insert the spline in a groove, and line up the other panel. Clamp panel in place.

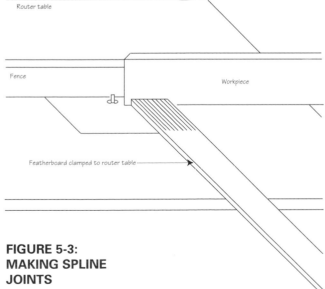

Router table

Fence

Workpiece

Featherboard clamped to router table

**FIGURE 5-3:
MAKING SPLINE
JOINTS**

By far, the easiest, quickest way to join a panel is with a biscuit joiner. The chief advantage of the biscuit joiner is that you only need to have a flat bottom and a square edge to accurately join two edges.

MAKING BISCUIT JOINTS

STEP 1
Mark the Joint

Like the dowel joint, you mark the position where you want the biscuit to go on both boards.

STEP 2
Cut the Joint

Line the biscuit joiner up with the marks and cut the slots. The biscuit doesn't have to be in the exact middle of the workpiece.

STEP 3
Assemble the Joint

Glue the edges and the slot.

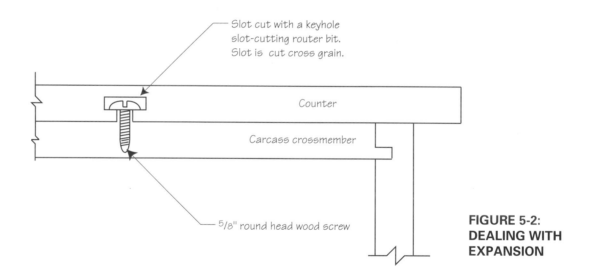

Slot cut with a keyhole slot-cutting router bit. Slot is cut cross grain.

Counter

Carcass crossmember

5/8" round head wood screw

FIGURE 5-2: DEALING WITH EXPANSION

FINISHING PANELS

Once your panels are assembled and the glue has dried, hand plane one surface of each panel so it will lie flat, and then surface them flat and smooth. I take my panels to a local trophy shop because my glued-up panels are almost always larger than my 12" planer can handle, and the trophy shop has a 36"-wide abrasive planer.

DEALING WITH EXPANSION

Solid-wood carcass construction proceeds much like plywood construction except you must allow for cross-grain expansion. I deal with this expansion by building solid-wood carcasses with upper and lower rails rather than full-width crosspieces, as shown in the Shaker-style center unit on page 65. Then I bury the heads of screws in slots cut with a keyhole-cutting router bit, as shown in the drawing above. This allows the board to be supported in one direction but still expand and contract in the other direction. There are a number of hardware fixes that allow you to attach tops to carcasses and allow for expansion, too.

BUILDING FRAME-AND-PANEL CARCASSES

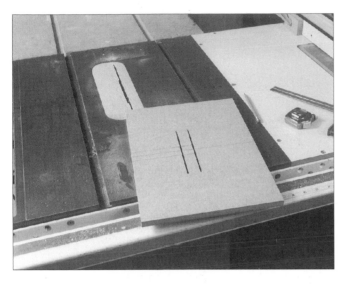

Frame-and-panel carcasses are built in much the same fashion as raised-panel doors. Central to frame-and-panel carcasses is the use of mortise-and-tenon joinery rather than the cope-and-stile joinery you find in well-built doors. In this chapter, I'll show you how to cut mortise-and-tenon joints; read chapter six for details about making panels.

Frame-and-panel carcasses minimize the expansion-contraction cycle that makes solid-wood construction more challenging. If the panel is a square of ¼" plywood, as in the Shaker doors, you can build a nice, tight fit that won't explode, and if you build raised-panel carcass members, the loose fit of the raised panels in the lengthwise groove of the frame members allows the solid-wood panels to expand and contract.

BUILD THE LEG BOTTOM MORTISING JIG

STEP 1
Cut the Sides

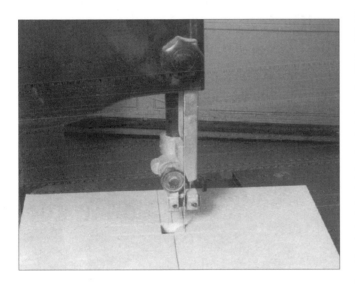

Build the mortising jig for the leg bottoms by cutting two parallel saw-kerfs in a piece of ½" MDF. First, adjust the fence so the saw blade will cut to the center of a piece of 14" x 10" MDF, as shown in the drawing on page 86. Clamp a stop block to the fence so the work-piece is stable, and raise the blade until it cuts a kerf about 2" long through the top of the workpiece. Lower the blade again, and move the fence one inch to the right. Raise the blade again, and cut a similar-length kerf.

STEP 2
Cut the Ends

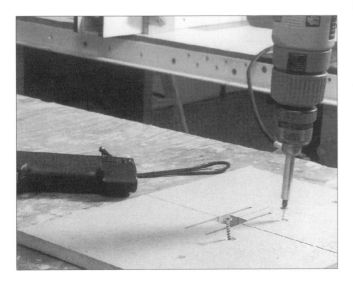

Once the two kerfs are sawn, draw center lines longitudinally and horizontally through the MDF workpiece. Draw lines ⁹⁄₁₆" from the horizontal center line and perpendicular to the saw-kerfs so you mark out an exact square with 1⅛" sides. Cut out the waste from the square hole by crosscutting along one horizontal center line until you reach the waste.

STEP 3
Trim and Square the Edges

Carefully trim the hole to size, and then screw a straight-edge on the underside of the jig, locating it parallel to the saw-kerf and such that the center line of the square hole is aligned with the center line of the leg bottom.

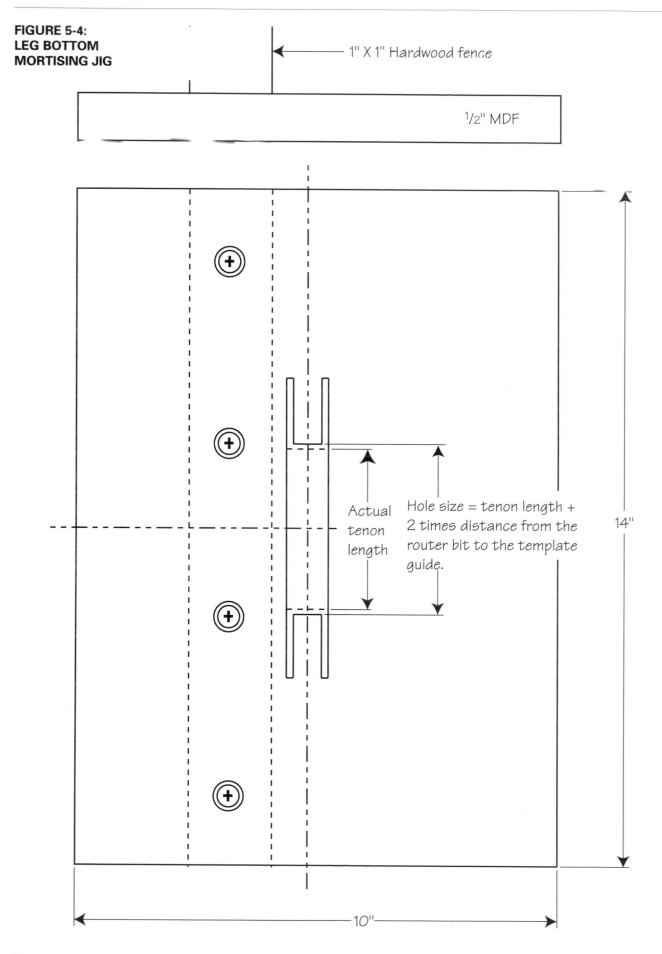

**FIGURE 5-4:
LEG BOTTOM
MORTISING JIG**

1" X 1" Hardwood fence

1/2" MDF

Actual tenon length

Hole size = tenon length + 2 times distance from the router bit to the template guide.

14"

10"

USING THE LEG BOTTOM MORTISING JIG

STEP 1

Rout a Practice Mortise

Attach a template guide to your plunge router. Here I'm using a solid carbide ½" double-fluted mortising bit in my 1½" horsepower Porter Cable router. Now clamp a piece of scrap the same thickness as the leg bottom and rout a practice mortise. You want to rout ¾" deep.

STEP 2

Check Depth

Check for proper depth and make sure the mortise is on center with the leg bottom. Mark how much material needs to be removed on the tenon on the bottom of a leg, and then rout all the mortises in the leg bottoms.

STEP 3

Cut Tenons

Once the mortises are done, rout a tenon to size on a piece of scrap so you can test fit your joint. As before, make needed adjustments and then rout the tenons. You can either pare the tenon corners round or chop the round corners square with a sharp chisel.

SHAPING THE RAILS

To shape the rail, lay out center points for the holes, as shown in the drawing below. Bore these holes on the drill press, and then make long parallel cuts on the table saw using the same technique as cutting the saw-kerfs for the mortising jigs. Remember that the kerf is longer on the bottom side. After you've sawn the majority of the saw-kerf, finish cutting out the rail's mission-style shape on the band saw or, if you're very steady, with a handsaw. A Japanese ripsaw would be perfect for this job. Sand the sawn edges smooth, and then round over or bevel the edges as per your preference. I routed mine round with a ¼" roundover bit.

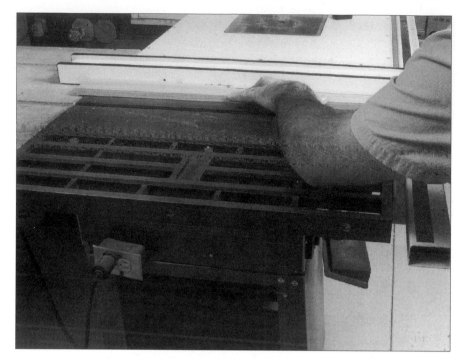

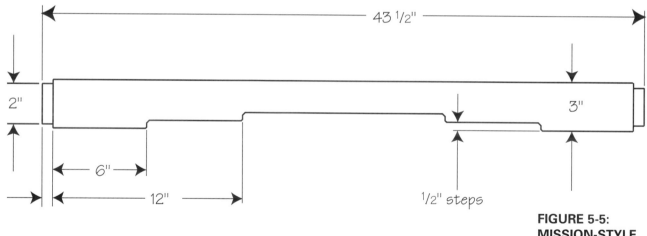

43 ½"

2"

3"

6"

12"

½" steps

**FIGURE 5-5:
MISSION-STYLE
RAIL**

MAKING THE LEG MORTISING JIG

STEP 1

Cut the Sides

Now make the mortising jig for the leg mortises in the same fashion as for the leg bottoms, but this time make the distance between the outside edges of the saw-kerfs the same size as the outer diameter of the template guide.

STEP 2

Mark the Ends

Mark how long you want the mortise to be and its center line on the face of the leg where you're going to rout the mortise. I drew a 2" space located ½" from the top of the leg to accommodate my 3"-wide rail. Once you establish the mortise length on the leg, align the center line of the jig with the center line of the mortise and transfer the end points of the mortise to the MDF surface. I inserted a ¼" solid carbide, double-fluted mortising bit into my plunge router. With the router turned off, turn the router upside down and plunge the baseplate down so the bit shoves up through the template guide about ¼" or so, and measure the distance from the edge of the guide to the edge of the bit. Add this amount, about ³⁄₁₆", to each of the two lines marking the end points of the mortise on the MDF jig.

STEP 3

Cut the Ends

Trim the leg mortise hole with a saber, coping, scroll or band saw. Mark the center line of the mortise on the interior sides of the hole, and then align these marks with the center lines of the mortise you've marked on the workpieces, as shown in the drawing on page 90.

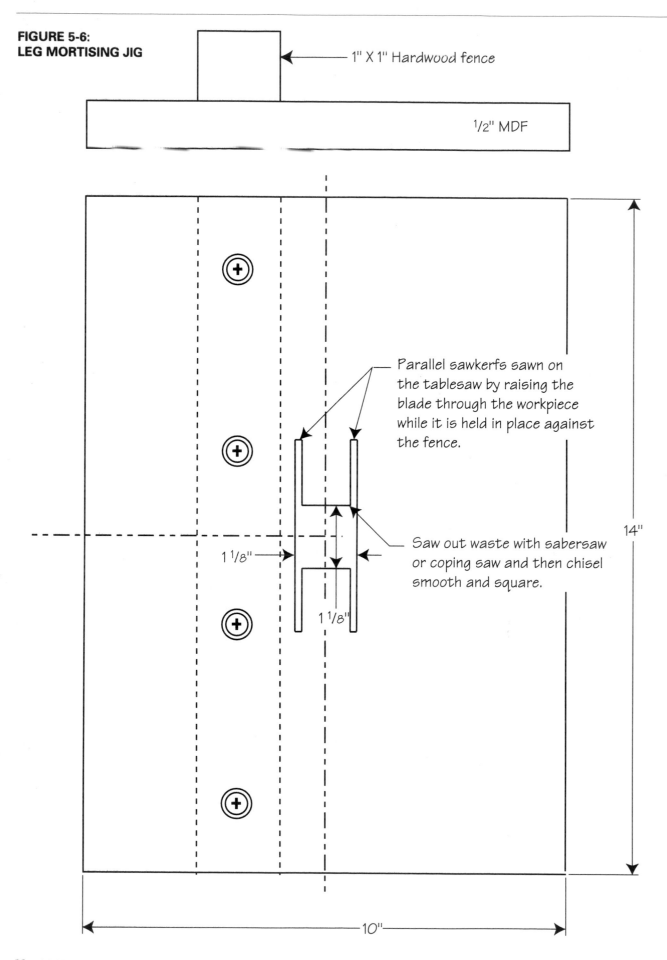

**FIGURE 5-6:
LEG MORTISING JIG**

1" X 1" Hardwood fence

1/2" MDF

Parallel sawkerfs sawn on
the tablesaw by raising the
blade through the workpiece
while it is held in place against
the fence.

Saw out waste with sabersaw
or coping saw and then chisel
smooth and square.

1 1/8"

1 1/8"

14"

10"

CUTTING THE LEG MORTISES

Lock Leg and Jig

Clamp the jig and leg in a vise, and then use a bar or C-clamp to lock the assembly together safely, as shown in the photo above.

Rout the Mortise

Rout the mortise in the same fashion as the leg bottom. You may need to vacuum the mortise before your final pass, as a mortise the same width as your router bit doesn't clear out as well as a double-wide mortise.

CUTTING THE RAIL TENONS

Cut the Shoulder

Score the shoulder of the tenon on the table saw with the blade raised just ⅛" to prevent tear-out, or eliminate the tear-out by pushing the workpiece through the cut with a piece of scrap. I like to put a pad of three Post-it notes on the surface to be routed and then whittle away at the tenon one pass at a time until I get a perfect fit.

Trim the Tenon

Trim the tenon to size. Use the band saw if you've got a lot to trim. Here I'm using a Japanese dovetail saw to trim the tenon to size.

Finish the Tenon

Either chisel the tenon round to fit the round mortises or chop the mortises square with a chisel. I left the mortises round because I didn't have a chisel small enough for the ¼"-wide mortise.

CHANGING SHAPES

Each of these designs is adjustable: You can make changes to the depth, height and width of each piece, but the overall rectilinear shape is immutable. The one concession I will allow, however, is that you may want to build an L-shaped unit to fit into a corner, and that implies that the center unit of the three-piece entertainment center is triangular. It is more difficult to build triangular-shaped units, but it is possible, and the inherently larger unit is especially useful for fitting a larger television into its upper carcass. My take on how to build this center unit for a corner is shown in the drawing on page 93. You could also make the argument that the wardrobe-on-chest entertainment centers are amenable to corners, too—corner cupboards are the stuff of country kitchens after all—but I haven't built such a unit and therefore plans for making such a transition are not included.

CHANGING SIZES

The first things you'll need to consider when you're deciding which design to build are the size and features of the room and the number and size of the electronic components you want to put in the entertainment center. Why is that important? Because you may want to alter the dimensions of the various components of the entertainment center you're going to build. So get out some graph paper and draw out the floor plan of the room at a 1" = 1' scale, and then sketch out a rectangle that represents the wall against which you're going to put the entertainment center. Now make a photocopy of these sketches, and on the

photocopy, sketch in, to scale, the entertainment center features you want to use.

As designed, these entertainment centers range from 76" to 86" in height. You will probably want to maintain a minimum of 3" of clearance above the unit for installation and best appearance in the room. Will one of these designs fit, or will you need to modify carcass height? Now imagine the patter of little feet through the room and how the doors and windows open. Does everything work right? Consider how your furniture will work in the room once the entertainment center is there. Does your recliner still stretch out? Is there still room for that ottoman? While you're measuring and drawing, note any baseboards or crown moldings that will prevent the entertainment center from sitting flush against the wall, and while you're at it, check the walls, floor and ceiling for squareness, too. Stretch a tape across the doorways and think about how you're going to get these big carcass units into the room and assembled. Note all existing electrical outlets and phone lines, and think about whether you need additional electrical/video/stereo/telecommunications service. Now is the time to do this head scratching, of course, because any mistakes you discover at this point don't cost extra, but you'll lose time and money if you discover mistakes later.

Once you've thought out all the kinks about room configurations, make a list of the electronics gear you want to stow, the books and bric-a-brac you want to house, and consider where you've got to alter the design to house some of this stuff. For example, while I've designed the three-piece units and the wardrobe-on-chest models to accommodate up to a 35" television, I'd want to consider how much that

behemoth weighed and whether I'd need to beef up my lower carcass before I actually built it. Figure out where you want to put the VCR, how you want to store the CDs, audiotapes and other paraphernalia. As you do so, it will become clearer how you will need to modify the basic design to suit your particular needs.

As a final admonition, consider how much everything will weigh. Few things are more disconcerting to woodworkers or homeowners than sagging shelves or carcasses. As you expand component size and increase load, you must consider the limits of material strength and the strength of your design. I routinely brace all ¾" plywood and MDF shelves over 30" in length, as shown in the drawing at top right. I let ¾" hardwood shelving go to 36" before I apply bracing. Furthermore, the wider the shelf and the more weight the shelf will bear, the thicker the brace will need to be.

As you make design changes, figure out how each change affects each part of the design. Photocopy the assembly drawing and materials list of the design you're interested in. Recalculate the dimensions of each affected part, and enter those dimensions on the materials list and the drawings.

Remember also that these changes will have an aesthetic effect. Try photocopying several copies of the design you are interested in, and try to visualize the results of enlarging or reducing the size of the design by cutting and pasting portions of the design on top of the original drawing. I think you will find there are definite limits beyond which the Shaker, mission or country styles cannot be successfully pushed but that you also have a considerable range of choice in customizing your entertainment center. Good luck and send me pictures.

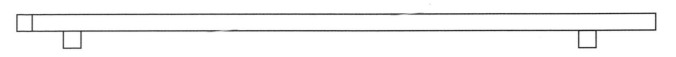

3/4" plywood shelf reinforced with 1/4" X 1 1/2" edging

FIGURE 5-8: REINFORCING SHELVES

3/4" plywood shelf edged with 3/4" hardwood and reinforced with 3/4" square hardwood cleats

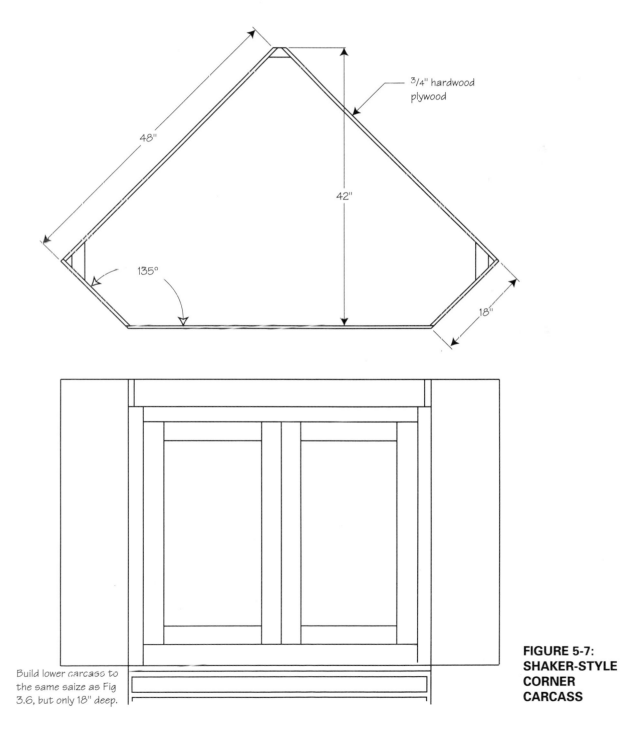

3/4" hardwood plywood

48"

42"

135°

18"

Build lower carcass to the same saize as Fig 3.6, but only 18" deep.

FIGURE 5-7: SHAKER-STYLE CORNER CARCASS

CHAPTER SIX

BUILDING CABINET DOORS

Cabinet doors are the focal point of your entertainment center and provide some of the most important vehicles to carry the chosen style's motif to the viewer. In that sense, then, their appearance, in terms of both design and craft, is critical. If you are changing the size of any of the entertainment center components, experiment with the proportion of door members to find the optimal relationship between cabinet opening, rail, stile and panel sizes.

SELECTING FRAME MATERIALS

The first step in building any door is to select appropriate materials. You must contemplate just what you want to convey by the door, whether it's the simplicity of the Shakers or the importance of line in a mission piece or whether you just want to highlight some remarkably figured wood. Regardless of your purpose, however, you want little or no figure at all for the stiles and rails, and unlike the face frames where flat-sawn wood works best, I find that vertical-grain wood works best for the door frames. In selecting wood in this fashion, I end up wasting quite a bit of wood, as shown in the photo at right. Although I regret making such unthrifty decisions, I often find use for the remnants in drawer construction.

ROUGH-CUT THE PIECES

After selecting the pieces for the doors, chop them out on the chop saw or radial arm saw and then mill them to final size. Do your best millwork, jointing, planing and crosscutting these pieces as squarely as possible. Remember, even slight error will multiply viciously and come back to bite you later. Always mill wood even if it's been surfaced prior to delivery. Never assume squareness or flatness in a workpiece.

SELECTING PANEL MATERIALS

Earlier, when I'd selected the material for the back panels of the carcasses from the 4' x 8' panels of ¼" ply-

wood, I took particular care to reserve the best figure for door panels for the Shaker-style doors. This is all book-matched vertical-grain cherry without much figure, consistent with the simple Shaker preferences. I had been hoarding some highly figured curly maple for the country-style doors, and I matched grain and hue for passable raised panels. Ideally, I would have selected some 6/4 material and resawed it for the panels so each door was a mirror image of the other, but I didn't have access to a big band saw. For the glass doors, I developed a simple pattern I thought carried the mission-style motif and then visited a couple of glass suppliers in the area. One, a typical glass supplier, could have etched the design into the glass, but the other, a stained-glass artisan, was able to build the leaded-glass windows I desired. I had to rout the groove in the door frame members, as described on page 96, to ⁵⁄₁₆" to accommodate the leaded glass.

CUTTING LIST—COUNTRY-STYLE ARMOIRE

Pediment			
Pediment Molding		¾" x 3" x 96"	Maple
Pediment Molding		¾" x 3" x 96"	Maple
Upper Carcass			
(A) Carcass Side	(2)	¾" x 22¼" x 43½"	Birch Plywood
(B) Top & Bottom	(2)	¾" x 22¼" x 42¼"	Birch Plywood
(C) Face-Frame Sides	(2)	¾" x 2" x 43½"	Maple
(D) Face-Frame Crosspieces	(2)	¾" x 2" x 38¾"	Maple
Country-Style Door			
(E) Upper Rail	(2)	¾" x 6" x 13½"	Maple
(F) Stile	(4)	¾" x 3" x 41⅛"	Maple
(G) Lower Rail	(2)	¾" x 3½" x 13½"	Maple
(H) Panel	(2)	¾" x 13½" x 35¼"	Maple
Counter and Base			
(I) Side	(4)	4/4" x 5" x 26"	Maple
(J) Front	(2)	4/4" x 5" x 47"	Maple
(K) Center Panel	(2)	4/4" x 22" x 37"	Medium-Density Fiberboard (MDF)
Lower Carcass			
(L) Side Rail	(4)	5/4" x 3½" x 18"	Maple
(M) Carcass Stile	(4)	8/4" x 4" x 30"	Maple
(N) Side Panel	(2)	¾" x 18" x 24"	Maple
(O) Rear Stile	(2)	¾" x 3½" x 41¾"	Maple
(P) Rear Panel		¼" x 24" x 41¾"	Birch Plywood
(Q) Side Slide Support	(4)	⅝" x 2" x 22"	Maple
(R) Lower Side Slide Support	(2)	⅝" x 3½" x 17"	Maple
(S) Front Center Stiles	(3)	1⅛" x 1⅛" x 9¼"	Maple
(T) Center Slide Support	(3)	1⅛" x 1⅛" x 22"	Maple
(U) Front Rail	(4)	1⅛" x 1⅛" x 41¾"	Maple
(V) Rear Center Stile		1⅛" x 1⅛" x 30"	Maple
Drawer			
(W) Drawer Front	(6)	¾" x 7⅞" x 21"	Maple
(X) Drawer Front & Back	(12)	½" x 7⅛" x 19½"	Maple
(Y) Drawer Side	(12)	½" x 7⅛" x 19⅜"	Maple
(Z) Drawer Bottom	(6)	¼" x 19⅛" x 19¼"	Maple
Foot			
Foot	(6)	8/4" x 5" x 10½"	Maple

CUTTING TONGUE-AND-GROOVE JOINTS FOR PANEL AND GLASS

STEP 1
Mark the Pieces

Match the rails and stile for each door with comparable grain and hue. Put identification marks on one face of each piece so you'll be able to keep these alike parts together.

STEP 2
Cut the Groove

Cut the groove first by whatever means you have available. I used the table saw or the router with a grooving bit and then ripped or grooved with one pass from each face of the workpiece to assure the groove was exactly on center.

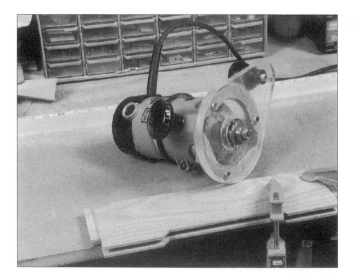

STEP 3
Cut the Tongue

Finally, the only fussy bit of the joint was cutting the tongue on the router table.

ROUTING RAISED-PANEL DOOR JOINERY

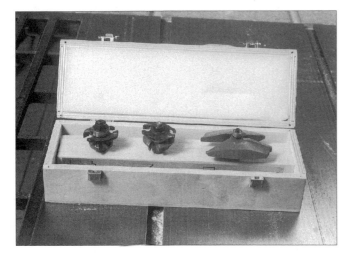

There are many commercially available door-making bits for the router, if you want to cut a little fancier beading than the tongue-and-groove joint.

LAYING OUT AND CUTTING THE DOORS

STEP 1

Draw the Curve

To draw the curve at the top of the panel, salvage the cutout you had leftover when you cut the curved part of the upper door stile. Bore a tight pencil hole ⅜" from the edge. Now run that edge along the curve's arc, and the pencil will draw the line for the slightly larger arc you need for the panel.

STEP 2

Cut Shoulders

Cut the panel shoulders on the table saw sled with stop blocks in place to limit the length of the shoulder, and then cut the curved edge on the band saw. Finally, sand the edge smooth and true.

Shape the Profile

Take care when shaping with a large-diameter panel-raising bit. This particular bit I'm using here is 3½" in diameter. I have mounted it in my 3½" horsepower variable speed Porter Cable fixed-base router, and the router in turn is mounted in my solid and heavy router table. I have screwed the ⅜" acrylic base to the router table, and I have clamped the fence securely to the tabletop.

Set the router to the lowest speed, in this case 10,000 rpm. Note how I am taking shallow cuts, ⅛" or less at a time, and that I'm using the fence as a fulcrum to slowly advance the workpiece into the bit to trim off the majority of the waste at the top of the curved workpiece.

Cut Straight Sides

I use the fence in this fashion to remove most of the waste from the workpiece until I get to final depth for the straight portions of the panel. Then I remove the fence and add a stop block as a fulcrum to advance the partially cut curved portion into the bit until the edge rides against the ball-bearing guide on the top of the bit. Now I can advance the curve into the bit and make the final cut. Incidentally, make the cross-grain cuts first and then the with-grain cuts. In this fashion, you will cut off any tear-out after you've made the cross-grain cuts.

ASSEMBLING AND FINISHING THE DOORS

Assembly is easy for the simple plywood-paneled doors. Essentially you just glue up the joints so the squeeze-out occurs where you can readily deal with it after it dries. Since you are planing these Shaker-style doors after assembly, squeeze-out is not a big concern. Squareness should not be an issue either, as the joinery should keep the door square.

ASSEMBLING GLASS-PANEL DOORS

Door assembly proceeds much like the plywood-paneled doors except you must be careful with squeeze-out as any excess glue cannot be removed mechanically with the glass in place. For the mission-style doors, I recommend finishing the frame members prior to assembly, taking care not to finish the joint components, and then assembling after one or two coats of finish. In this fashion, any squeeze-out will not adhere to a surface and will chip off fairly easily.

ASSEMBLING RAISED-PANEL DOORS

The most problematic door is the raised-panel door. Because you are inserting a big hunk of wood in the middle of a door, you know that cross-grain expansion is going to be a problem. I anticipated about a $\frac{3}{16}$" summer-winter expansion-contraction coefficient and consequently left a $\frac{1}{4}$" difference between the panel size and the interior dimension from the bottom of the groove in one rail to the bottom of the groove in the other. More importantly, I needed to be more careful with the glue than with either of the other two types of

doors. Because the panel needs to be free to expand and contract in the groove, you cannot allow the glue to come in contact with the panel and prevent free expansion and contraction. Furthermore, as with the mission-style doors, you cannot run this door through the planer, so after assembly, you will need to deal with squeeze-out by hand. And finally, since finish can act like a glue, you must finish the raised-panel door members before assembly.

For the larger doors, I backed up the stub tenons with dowels; the short mortise-and-tenon joints are not strong enough for the heavier doors.

For the flat-panel doors as in the Shaker-style entertainment centers, I was able to take the glued-up doors right to my friends who have a 36"-wide abrasive planer. I had to surface the raised-panel doors to size without the panels because they project about ⅛" proud of the door's stiles and rails and that meant surfacing with unglued joints.

CHAPTER SEVEN

MAKING DRAWERS

Dovetails are the hallmark of a cabinetmaker's skill. Even minimally well educated shoppers know to yank open a drawer and look at how a drawer was constructed as an estimate of quality of the entire piece of furniture.

However, when you are actually faced with the stack materials needed to build drawers, you soon realize it takes more than sophisticated taste to saw, chop and pare the needed dovetail joints by hand. In this chapter, I show you how to cut three types of dovetails, as shown in the drawing at right, with a router and a couple of commercially available jigs for quick, easy and accurate drawer production.

Make sure you mill the wood for the drawers with our usual concern for craftsmanship. Heed my usual admonition and make certain all surfaces are flat, all edges square and all like pieces the same dimension. Use a sled and stop blocks as in the photo below, to make sure.

Offset dovetail

Rabbeted offset dovetail

Through dovetail

Tongue and groove

Rabbeted tongue and groove

FIGURE 7-1: DRAWER JOINTS

CUTTING HALF-BLIND DOVETAILS

The Sears dovetailing jig I use allows me to cut both pins and dovetails at the same time by positioning the drawer side and front (or back) in the correct relationship to one another.

STEP 1

Clamp the Workpieces

Once the workpieces are locked into position with metal crossbars, the comblike guide is positioned atop the jig. Note that the crossbar is equipped with knobs that tighten the bar against the workpiece. I have replaced these with ordinary hex nuts. After replacing these knobs with nuts, I also backed up this clamping mechanism with bar clamps. Also notice I have clamped a piece of scrap along the edge of the top workpiece. This prevents tear-out.

STEP 2

Cut the Dovetails

The guide mounted on the bottom of the Sears router slides down between the fingers of the jig's comb while the router bit, a Sears #25505½" carbide-tipped bit, cuts the dovetails.

Note that the pins are actually rounded on one end to fit into the half-round shape left by the router bit.

CUTTING RABBETED HALF-BLIND DOVETAILS

The rabbeted half-blind dovetailed drawer starts out just like the half-blind drawer; you just cut the half-blind dovetails like you did in the sequence above. The comb-shaped router guide is positioned in place, and then the dovetails are routed in the same fashion as with the off-set dovetails.

DRAWER-FACE JOINERY

The cutting of the joinery for the drawer face proceeds much as the half-blind joint except that you must cut each half of the joint separately, and when cutting the dovetails in the drawer face, you must position the edge of the rabbet in the same place as the vertical face of the jig, with the rabbeted lip of the drawer front jutting out farther. You still position the drawer face against the factory-set stops as with the offset dovetails.

With the rabbeted half-blind dovetail, however, on the drawer front, you must first cut a rabbet all around the perimeter of the drawer front. Here, I'm cutting that rabbet on the router table with the drawer face up.

To position the drawer side in the correct position, cut a piece of scrap the same width and thickness as the rabbet on the drawer front.

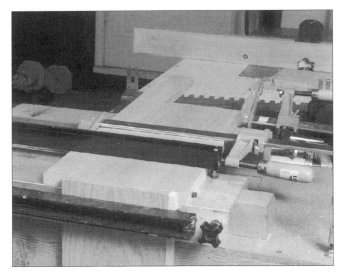

Position the side in place with the piece of scrap located between the stop pin and the workpiece. Clamp a piece of scrap the same thickness as the drawer front in back of the side so tear-out will be minimized and you can adjust the side to the correct height.

Rout the pins in the same fashion as routing the off-set dovetails.

Assemble the drawers, and with any luck, you should have a perfect fit.

CUTTING THROUGH DOVETAILS WITH A KELLER DOVETAILING JIG

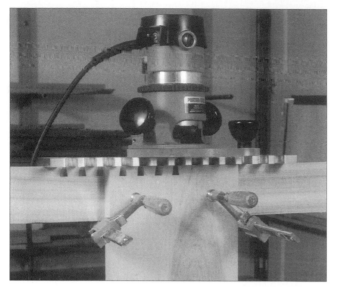

Both templates are positioned in exactly the same fashion. You cut the dovetails first.

After you cut the dovetails, you hold the dovetailed board atop the end grain of the part that will have the pins and carefully scribe the position of a pin onto that end grain. From there, it's a simple matter to position the template in place. Make sure you align one of the metal teeth of the template exactly on top of the scribed pin position. Because you're using a pattern bit, what you see is what you get once you rout the pin.

A nest of drawers is a pleasurable thing to get into, provided you're equipped with a dovetail jig and router. As shown in the bottom left photo, the cherry and maple drawers are sporting offset dovetails perfect for the Shaker-style drawers, the two oak drawers are showing off their rabbeted offset dovetails for the mission-style entertainment center, and the country-style maple drawers with the through dovetails are ready for trimming and fitting with a separate drawer face. The first two were cut with a Sears model 2579 ($60) dovetail jig, while the last six drawers were cut with the Keller model 1601 dovetail jig (about $200).

The Keller dovetail jig is a simple, reliable, no-fuss means of cutting through dovetails. It is a two-part jig with one straight comblike template for cutting the dovetails and another comblike template with 7° angled teeth that allow you to cut the pins. The straight template is for the dovetail bit, while the angled template uses a ⅝" x ½" pattern bit to cut the pins.

Cut the Bottom Groove

Cut a rabbet ¼" wide, ¼" deep and located ¼" from the bottom edge of the drawer to accommodate the ¼" plywood drawer bottom.

Clamp the Drawer

Dado a comblike apparatus as shown at left, and then clamp it across the dovetails so the pins can project upward beyond the plane of the drawer side.

Sand the Drawers

After the glue dries, belt sand the drawers. Make sure you sand only from the far end of the drawer to the middle or you will chip out the near end's dovetails.

CHAPTER EIGHT

INSTALLING HARDWARE

Hardware is what makes cabinets work. This is particularly true for entertainment centers because we ask them to do more. In addition to the door hinges, drawer slides, handles, pulls, catches and knobs that regular kitchen cabinets require, entertainment centers need extension slides for the television to swing out and side to side. They must offer vented spaces to store the various electronic components and a system for housing the storage media for those components. Electricity needs to get to the electronic organisms within, and you need to manage the cabling that routes and meters that electricity. There is a host of work to do, so let's get on with it.

INSTALLING DRAWER SLIDES

STEP 1

Make the Jig

Make a slide guide to hold the slide in position while you screw it to the frame member. I just screw a piece of ¼" plywood to a piece of hardwood with about a ¼" lip of plywood overhanging the hardwood's width.

STEP 2

Drill Pilot Holes

To use the slide guide, butt the hardwood edge against the underside of the inner rail, and position the slide against the parallel plywood edge. Drill pilot holes and screw in fasteners while holding the slide in position with one hand.

INSTALLING SLIDES IN BOTTOM RAILS

STEP 1

Bring Side Flush to Rail

For the bottom inner rails, I simply screwed a ³⁄₁₆" piece of scrap to make a continuous surface in the same plane as the front and rear vertical rails.

STEP 2

Mark Holes

Because of this, however, my slide guide was not set at the right dimension, and rather than making another jig, I used a combination square adjusted to the appropriate height to position the rail.

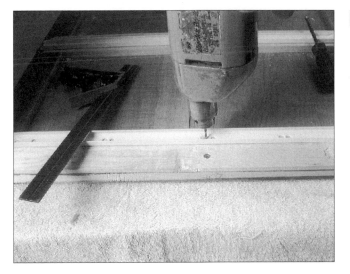

STEP 3

Drill the Holes

At the correct height, mark and drill the holes.

MAKING AND INSTALLING DRAWER ORGANIZERS

The self-adhesive sticky pads these videotape racks sport are inadequate. I cut double-sided carpet tape for better adhesion.

You can cut these plastic drawer organizers to fit with woodworking tools using the same techniques you use for wood.

To make my own organizers for diskettes, CDs and audiotapes, I first made a ¼" plywood sled to fit under the auxiliary fence I installed on the miter gauge.

Using this miter gauge accessory, I was able to make tear-out-free saw-kerfs and space them regularly using the fence as a movable stop block.

The 3½" computer diskettes fit well in a regular ⅛" saw-kerf, while the CDs require tinkering with a dado head for the right fit. The diskettes read fairly well from above if you cut the kerf at an 18° angle. Everything else seemed to work best when the dado held them vertically. The videotapes looked really clunky with wooden organizers, so I bought the plastic injection-molded ones.

INSTALLING POCKET DOOR HARDWARE

Bore the holes for the hinge cups in the door using the drill press with a 35mm Forstner bit in the chuck. Locate the holes in accordance with the instructions provided by the manufacturer.

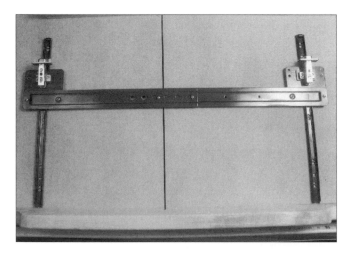

The assembled slide apparatus has two slides that are mounted parallel to one another. Two roller carriages travel back and forth along the slides and are connected to one another by an adjustable follower strip. The European-style cup hinges clip onto the mounting plates, which are screwed to the carriages.

There are several real advantages to this pocket door hardware. One, it lets you adjust the door in all three dimensions for a perfect fit. Two, it works for European-style cabinetry, conventional flush-fit face-frame doors, as shown here in these Shaker-style cabinets, or it will also allow you to install overhung doors on the face frame. Furthermore, this is the only solution for entertainment center construction that allows you to move the doors out of the way for video viewing.

I use a piece of wood to locate each spacer equally from the top or bottom.

After installing the cup hinges on the door, I clip the door to the slide assembly and slide the door into the face-frame opening. I mark the screw holes in two places with an awl and then drill the screw holes. Then I disassemble the door from the slide assembly and install the slide with just the two screws holding each of the slides in position. Next I clip on the door again and test it for fit. Since it fits well, I screw in the rest of the slide screws, but if necessary, I make the needed adjustments by choosing different screw holes.

I build this three-sided box for the VCR to sit under, and on top, I mount the extension slide that the television sits on. I used the same through dovetails that I used for the country-style drawers (see chapter seven for dove-tailing details) and recommend dovetails as the best joint for this work if the box is made of solid hardwood. You could also cut dadoes, as illustrated in the photos at left, which will work for boxes built of plywood or hardwood, but I would back up the joint and glue with screws. Remember, you're going to have a 200-pound television sitting on top of this box, and you don't want it squashed.

INSTALLING EXTENSION SLIDES

I used connector bolts to fasten the box to the carcass of the entertainment center. These screw into metal slugs that are positioned horizontally through a second hole that's bored at 90° to the bolt holes. You don't bore this hole all the way through, and, therefore, the method of fastening is hidden from view.

Assembled, the extension slide lets you move the television forward or back and swing it right or left.

Hardware makes entertainment centers work. Here, the Shaker-style entertainment center doors slide back into their "pockets," revealing the television, the extension slide and the VCR box. A similar box hanging over the television can house stereo equipment, or a larger (up to 35") television can fit within.

INSTALLING KNIFE HINGES

STEP 1
Trim the Doors

Trim the doors so there is the same fit between all members of the door-door frame assembly. Note the cardboard-card combinations sticking out between the doors and frame.

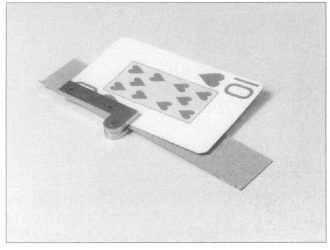

STEP 2
Measure the Hinge

Determine how much space there is between the two blades of the hinge. Here, I've determined that a piece of cardboard from a tablet and a playing card make for the ideal fit.

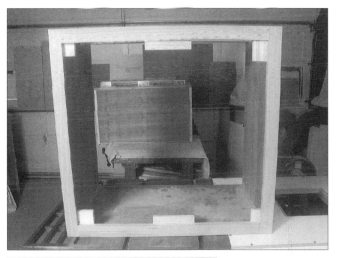

STEP 3
Install Strips to Hold Door

Screw six pieces of scrap wood to the inside of the face frame with drywall screws to hold the doors flush with the face frame.

STEP 4
Scribe the Line

Locate the end of the hinge by scribing a line with a knife on the inside of the face frame while holding the hinge in position. Though you can't see them in the photo, I am gauging the hinge's location against the vertical face-frame member with that piece of cardboard and the playing card.

Prepare for Routing Groove

Clamp a stop block on the face of the face frame to limit the length of the router travel, and clamp a ⅛"-thick piece of scrap to the inner edge of the vertical face frame.

Rout the Groove

Now insert a ⅜" x 1" rabbeting bit with a ¼" guide bearing into your router and rout the short ⅛"-deep groove that will become the fitted recess for the knife hinge. When you are done with all four hinge sites, you will have four short grooves all located in exactly the same location, all exactly ⅛" deep (exactly as deep as one blade of the hinge is thick) and all exactly the same width as the knife hinge.

Rout the Recess in the Doors

In the same fashion, use a stop block to limit the length of the groove on the doors, and rout the recess for the hinge on the doors. Watch for tear-out on the end grain. You may want to scribe a line across the door edge where the groove will end, or, if you're an experienced router user, try feeding the router from the edge toward the stop. Remember, this is a more dangerous procedure, and the bit will try to self-feed. Like the grooves you cut in the face frame, these are all exactly ⅛" deep and the same width as the knife hinge.

Drill the Holes

Drilling the inner screw holes is tricky because they are located so close to the vertical face-frame member. I have a little hand-cranked drill that lets me get in close.

CHAPTER NINE

FINISHING

Congratulations, you're in the homestretch. All of the components for your entertainment center are milled, machined and ready to be assembled. A couple of cautionary words: Slow down! Now is the time when extra care pays off. Even though you're getting anxious to complete your project (and it looks great), most woodworkers falter when it comes time to put a coat of finish on the project. A good rule of thumb is that it should take as long to finish your project as it does to build it.

Take your time. Remember, this thing is going to be hanging around your house for a long time, so be sure to fix all the little things that need fixing before you apply finish.

SURFACE PREPARATION

In order to get one of those great, glossy deep finishes you see in the magazines, you've got to build the perfect surface for it before a drop goes on the wood. What does that mean? First, alignment: Use a block plane and scraper to make joined surfaces and edges exactly in the same plane. One problem area is where the face frame attaches to the carcass. Because that veneer of hardwood is thin, go cautiously with the belt sander and block plane or you'll plane right through the veneer. I like a hand scraper for this job. When you use the belt sander on a narrow edge, clamp on a guide board so the sander doesn't rock unevenly across the workpiece. For long flat surfaces, the belt sander works wonders when you have a lot of material to remove(top left), but be careful, as you can gouge the workpiece very quickly. The little orbital sander is just about essential whenever you're tackling a substantial project. Hand sanding gets old fast. As you come across glue in tight corners, try using a chisel to remove it (bottom left), or a chisel plane works well, too. Use a hand scraper to remove glue from flat surfaces. When you've gone over all of the components of the entertainment center, begin filling the gaps, splits, checks and other flaws you undoubtedly will find. There are a variety of products for filling the inevitable holes, flaws and outright errors you want to hide whether before finishing, between coats while finishing or after you've completed finishing. At this point I had to stain water-soluble filler with a black water-soluble stain to fill a really dark crevasse in my mission-style door. I had already put one coat of finish on and used two more after this. Now begin sanding with 120-grit sandpaper on the roughest parts of the wood, those areas where you didn't joint the table-sawn edge or where end grain is exposed. After sanding those troublesome areas, I sand with 180-grit paper throughout.

STAINING AND FILLING GRAIN

If you are using a small pored wood like maple or cherry, you may stain the wood at this point, after vacuuming and wiping the wood with a tack cloth. I used Deft's golden oak water-based wood stain on the maple country-style entertainment center, wiping off the residue several minutes after application. After drying overnight, I sand with a fine abrasive pad because the water-based stains tend to raise the grain a bit.

I did not stain the cherry Shaker-style entertainment center, but the mission-style oak entertainment center needed both filler and stain. I used a golden oak stain here, too, but in an oil-based mix from Colonial. I mixed the filler to stain at a two-to-one proportion until it was a thin, creamy consistency. I always have the paint store mix and shake up a new can of the filler before I take it home because the solids in the shelved can tend to settle into an impenetrable clump, and it can be a mess to try to stir at home. Advance slowly and cautiously until you know how long it takes the filler to dry when filling the grain. It's important to be methodical and not progress too far when filling the grain of big pored woods like the oak in the mission-style pieces. I like to proceed a couple of square feet at a time. In the middle left photo I've added an oil-based stain to the filler and have brushed on the filler in a thick, creamy layer. Next I've gone forward another couple of square feet, and you can see the difference in how the two surfaces appear. The first surface is beginning to cloud up, which is the first step in becoming totally dry, which you do not want to happen without further work. When the surface begins to dull, rub the filler/stain mix into the grain by rubbing in a circular motion. Now work the filler into the pores of the wood with burlap, working it in a circular motion and removing much of the filler. Apply another two-square-foot section of filler if you have time, monitor the second application and then wipe the first section, with the grain, taking care not to pull the filler out of the grain, but wiping the filler from the wood as much as possible.

The day after you filled the grain, sand down to wood level again by using abrasive pads and orbital sanders. In the photo at bottom left, you can see where I've rubbed off the filler residue on the left. This exercise quickly compels one to do a better job with the burlap the night before. Sand through 220-grit.

APPLYING FINISH

Apply the finish of your choice by rubbing, brushing or spraying it on. If you have access to spraying equipment, you may be able to spray your entertainment center over a weekend. This will minimize your finishing time when compared with brushing or rubbing on an oil finish, but there's a certain sensuous tedium you'll be missing, too.

Brushing a finish may be tedious if yours is a large entertainment center, but there's a satisfaction in brushing on a finish and methodically proceeding over all the surfaces until every square inch is covered. Although it is primarily designed for HVLP (high-volume, low-pressure) spraying, you can also brush on the water-based finish I used in this project. This finish was Sherwin William's Kem Var "W" W/R Conversion Varnish V84 V530 that uses a catalyst to harden the finish, Kem Var Catalyst, V66 V21. Although it is fairly benign, I wore a respiration mask when applying it. The finish does give off formaldehyde as it dries.

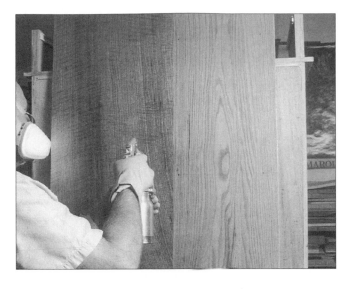

You'll never get a high-gloss finish with oil, but nothing's easier to apply. You simply spill a pool of tung oil on your project and rub it into the wood, wiping up the excess as you proceed. An oil finish doesn't protect the wood like a surface film you've sprayed or brushed on, but it has the advantage of being really simple to apply and it's infinitely repairable.

Between coats, slice off any drips, and then level this area with fine sandpaper. Regardless of whether you spray or brush, abrade the entire finish surface lightly between coats with the next higher grit sandpaper, steel wool or abrasive pad. Clean the surface with mineral spirits or lacquer thinner on a clean soft cloth or use a tack cloth. If you are using putty between coats of finish, apply it now. After you've attained an appropriately thick "skin" of finish, rub the finish to the gloss you desire.

If you are using a penetrating oil finish, rub it on with a soft cloth in accordance with the instructions on the can. Now stand back and admire.

CHAPTER TEN

SELECTING MATERIALS AND SUPPLIES

I will never understand the rationale for building with poor or inappropriate materials. As I wander through some of the worst cut-rate stores, I see fiberboard end tables and shelves sporting bound-to-bust joinery and the cheapest of hardware, all covered with photo-reproduced wood-grained plastic film. Argh, enough to gag a termite.

Of course, when you're building 10,000 units of anything, if you can save a nickel a unit, it adds up, but this kind of thrift doesn't make sense for real woodworkers or discerning customers. Help to rebuild the notion of value. Aim to build the best given the constraints of pocketbook, time, workshop and skill.

Not that there's anything wrong with alternate materials. Fiberboard and plastic laminates will prove perfect in some circumstances. In this chapter, I'll talk a bit about various materials and what they're good for and not so good for.

REAL WOOD

No doubt about it, there's nothing quite like wood as a building material. Genuine, durable, living, breathing wood is an extraordinary material. People have been whittling,

shaving, sawing, drilling and abrading it for tens of thousands of years. Its uses are manifold, all encompassing, profound and ubiquitous.

Nonetheless, wood is plagued with many problems: It rots, it warps, it is afflicted with an incredible range of color, strength, machinability, finishability and beauty. You must be well acquainted with a wood before you make design decisions about using it. The three woods I have chosen, maple, oak and cherry, are traditional cabinet woods, each highly appropriate for

the projects in this book. Stray from these recommendations only if you are knowledgeable about the alternates.

Even given these recommendations, however, you must make choices about individual pieces of these woods, choices you will live with for a long time. Choose only select-grade wood, even though you can get #1 common for $1 per foot. Discard any wood with visible flaws, or mill it for smaller pieces. Take time matching figure and grain.

PLYWOOD

The chief problem with real wood is its expansion and contraction in response to humidity. This makes for problems with furniture exploding. Plywood solves this problem and offers several other advantages. First, it is dependably flat with two parallel surfaces. This cuts down on your milling. Second, plywood is available in 4' x 8' sheets, and, consequently, you don't have to go to the bother of gluing up wide panels of hardwood. Third, it is uniformly of a high-grade surface, and often, highly figured wood is available.

Plywood has several disadvantages, too. It is difficult to work such large sheets. There is little screw-holding capacity in plywood edges. You have to face the edge grain with hardwood for it to look like hardwood throughout. Finally, the hardwood veneer is thin and can easily be sanded through unless you are careful.

Plywood is available in ¼", ⅜", ½", ⅝" and ¾" nominal sizes. Metric-sized plywood is available, too, but not readily so in the United States. Plywood is available as either veneer core or fiber core. I prefer the veneer core plywood.

OTHER SYNTHETIC WOOD PRODUCTS

Generally, most synthetic wood products are used in the construction trades, although several are commonly used in furniture construction, for better or worse. Medium density fiberboard (MDF) is one product I use extensively in my workshop for jig building and inexpensive counters and bases. It is a superior material for a base for laminates and veneers. It glues well, machines well and accepts paint well. In my experience, it does not take screws well. I also used some ¼" pegboard to make a hole-drilling jig for shelves for the three-piece entertainment centers.

GLUE

For the projects in this book, I experimented with a new glue, Excel's waterproof, gap-filling polyurethane glue, which I have found to be superior to the more traditional yellow glue, the aliphatic resin glue. Although I do not know about its long-term durability, in the short term, it is a most forgiving glue. It scrapes off easily, sands off cleanly, and the gap-filling feature of this glue will be a boon to all but the most talented woodworkers.

BISCUITS

There are many effective methods of edge joining pieces of wood together, but these little wafers of wood, or biscuits, as they are called, are the simplest, quickest and easiest method of doing so. They come in a variety of sizes and require a piece of portable power tool equipment, the biscuit joiner, to cut the needed biscuit slots.

FASTENERS

Drywall screws rank right up there with duct tape and routers when considering some of the great inventions of the twentieth century. I used 1", 1¼", 1½", 1⅝", 2" and 2½" drywall screws throughout these projects. Even though drywall screws are supposed to be self-tapping, I always drill a pilot hole and countersink the hole when screwing in hardwood.

Although you'll find that drywall screws make nails pretty much passé, you will need an array of finishing nails to finish this project. I keep ⅝" and ⅞" brads and 1¼" and 1½" finishing nails on hand.

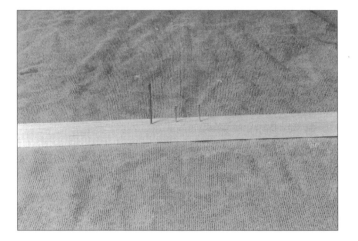

WOOD

BRISTOL VALLEY HARDWOODS
4054 Bristol Valley Rd.
Bristol, NY 14424
(800) 724-0132

HARDWOOD HEAVEN
1620 S. Third St.
Lincoln, NE 68501
(402) 477-5989

STEVE WALL LUMBER CO.
544 River Rd.
P.O. Box 287
Mayodan, NC 27027
(910) 427-0637

HARDWARE

WOODWORKER'S HARDWARE
P.O. Box 180
Sauk Rapids, MN 56379
(800) 383-0130

CUSTOM GLASS

THE PALACE GLASS CO.
416 S. Eleventh St.
Lincoln, NE 68508
(402) 476-9661

ROUTER STUFF

CMT TOOLS
310 Mears Boulevard
Oldsmar, FL 34677
(800) 531-5559

EAGLE
P.O. Box 1099
Chardon, OH 44024
(800) 872-2511

WOODHAVEN
5323 W. Kimberly
Davenport, IA 52806
(800) 344-6657

GENERAL WOODWORKING SUPPLIERS

GARRETT WADE
161 Avenue of the Americas
New York, NY 10013
(800) 221-2942

HIGHLAND HARDWARE
1045 N. Highland Ave., NE
Atlanta, GA 30306
(800) 241-6748

THE WOODWORKER'S STORE
4365 Willow Dr.
Medina, MN 55340
(800) 279-4441

TRENDLINES
135 American Legion Highway
Revere, MA 02151
(800) 767-9999

WILLIAM ALDEN
27 Stuart St.
Boston, MA 02116
(800) 249-8665

WOODCRAFT
210 Wood County Industrial Park
P.O. Box 1686
Parkersburg, WV 26102-1686
(800) 225-1153

WOODWORKER'S SUPPLY
1108 N. Glenn Rd.
Casper, WY 82601
(800) 645-9292

INDEX

INDEX